# Billings
## The City and The People

by Roger Clawson and Katherine A. Shandera

Published by
The Billings Gazette
and Montana Magazine

## Dedications

To Nancy Perry Larsen, who believed in a young writer before he did.
-R.C.

To Steve, Sarah, Annie and Laura, the best cheerleaders a writer ever had.
-K.S.

## Acknowledgments

To the many Billings residents and historians who gave me so much of their time, and who will find those long conversations reduced to a few lines of text—thank you.
-K.S.

**Library of Congress Cataloging-in-Publication Data**
Clawson, Roger.
    Billings : the city and the people / by
Roger Clawson & Katherine A. Shandera.
    p.  cm.
    Includes bibliographical references
    and index.
    ISBN 1-56037-037-8
    1. Billings (Mont.)--History. 2. Billings
(Mont.)--Geography.
    I. Shandera, Katherine A. II. Title.
F739.B5C53 1993
978.6'39--dc20 93-17652

Text pages 8-50 © 1993 Roger Clawson
Text pages 52-108 © 1993 Katherine
  A. Shandera
© 1993 American & World Geographic
  Publishing
© 1993 Billings Gazette
Designed by Joyce L. Mayer

**Top:** *MontanaFair.* JAMES WOODCOCK
**Above:** *Historic and comfortable.* KEITH SIMONSEN
**Title page:** *Downtown.* MICHAEL CRUMMETT

*Skipping the bright
fantastic at McKinley
Elementary.* JAMES WOODCOCK

**Front cover:** *Billings
looking from the rimrocks
south toward the Bighorn
Mountains.* CHARLIE BORLAND
**Back cover:** *Downtown
Billings at dusk.*
TOM DIETRICH

## About the Authors

*W*inner of several national awards as a newspaper
reporter and columnist, Roger Clawson is a free-lance
writer, and the author of four books on Montana
subjects.

*K*atherine A. Gilbertz Shandera is a free-lance writer
and editorial consultant. She is a third-generation dream
seeker who grew up in Wyoming on the ranch her
grandfather homesteaded in 1916. She and her husband
and children now live in Billings where they continue to
seek dreams of their own.

**Today:** *Billings looking east (aerial).* LARRY MAYER
**Yesterday:** *A pre-aviation "bird's eye" view of Billings, 1898.* COURTESY PARMLY BILLINGS LIBRARY

# Billings

## The City and the People

*Mural on the Koinonia Restaurant.*
JAMES WOODCOCK

# Foreword

The natural features of Billings are first to catch the visitor's eye:

The Rims, that majestic slab of sandstone that defines and keeps watch over the Yellowstone Valley.

The Yellowstone River, running swift and green through a tangle of graceful cottonwood trees, wild rose and the scent of mint.

The Beartooth Mountains set like sapphires to the south, the crown jewels of the Big Sky.

Wide, tree-lined streets, a casualness in the way that people walk and stop to talk on downtown corners.

Then, the visitor's focus narrows, seeing the thread of prosperity that adorns the city like lights on a Christmas tree. He marvels at the friendliness of the people here, the ready smiles, the eagerness to talk about their home, about Montana.

Visitors leave Billings with a pang of regret, nagged by the feeling that they haven't really seen the soul of this city, and there is a secret here, something that hides from the casual observer.

There *is*. From the beginning, from the time that the Crow and the Sioux and the Cheyenne gathered here on what the Crow called the Big Elk River, people have come to this place because it is better than the place they left. They came here because this city and this area promised them a better life than what they left behind. They stay here because Billings and Montana fulfill their promise.

And each of us here attempts to make this city even more magic. Private citizens mix their vision with the public sector to deliver this city ZooMontana and a park that will run along the Yellowstone River, revealing the deer and beaver and mink and more birds than most of us can count.

Billings gives each of us something special, and each of us attempts to give this city something special in return. That makes Billings the Magic City.

*Wayne Schile*
*Publisher,* Billings Gazette

LARRY MAYER

# BEFORE BILLINGS

by Roger Clawson

# Ice Age and Early Peoples

*Tipi rings on the south slopes of the Pryor Mountains.* JOHN REDDY

*M*ore than 40,000 years ago an unexplained climatic change triggered an Ice Age. Continental glaciers nearly three miles thick covered much of the Northern Hemisphere. The massive ice sheet captured much of the earth's water—12 million square miles of frozen, freshwater sea sprawled over North America, Europe, and Asia. Sea level plunged, and the newly-exposed land became grassy plains or tundra. Thus, a land bridge stretched from Asia to Alaska.

The Alaskan Peninsula, swelled by the addition of these lands, filled with new arrivals from Asia—both humans and beasts. But the great ice sheet prevented these immigrants from penetrating farther south for nearly 30,000 years.

About 12,000 to 18,000 years ago, Earth's climate changed once again and the glaciers began to retreat. As the ice sheet melted, the sea rose, drowning fishing villages and covering many of the ancient hunting camps and butchering sites. The warming weather and rising seas

*Pictographs by the "Big Shield Warriors," ancestors of the Shoshones, adorn the Indian Caves east of Billings.*
BOB ZELLAR

cut off both the mammoths and the hunters from the Old World.

As the shrinking ice sheet divided into two continental glaciers, a corridor appeared between them. Humans and beasts followed the grass and forage south. Roughly 10,000 years ago, Paleolithic hunters emerged from that corridor somewhere near the present site of Wolf Point, Montana. Their children and grandchildren fanned out to populate both American continents in a remarkably short time.

Virgin hunting territory stretched thousands of miles southward, filled with game that had never seen nor had any reason to fear human hunters. Evidence shows these peoples slew and butchered the woolly mammoth in the Yellowstone Valley.

Hunting must have been superb for a time. A Pleistocene bison, much larger than the bison that covered the prairies in historic times, was probably the mainstay of the early hunter's diet.

This wave of human hunters swept south, exterminating the mega-fauna and leaving behind an empty land. Extinction claimed the Pleistocene bison, great tortoises, the giant ground sloth, giant beaver and others.

The woolly mammoth disappeared; some scholars contend that the change in climate was too great. Most others agree, however, that human hunters—not a warming trend—spelled the end of the great American elephants. An animal with a five-year gestation and nursing period could not survive the hunting pressure of a human population that grew geometrically. In less than 400 years, anthropologists estimate, both North America and South America had densities of one person per square mile.

A prolonged drought—one lasting perhaps 6,000 years—may have delayed people's return to the Northern Plains. Eventually, early peoples developed farming in Mexico and Central America. The corn culture spread northward in two fans, one sprawling across the Southwest, the other covering the Southeast.

A Siouxian-speaking peo-

ple—ancestors of the Lakota and the Crow—branched again and again as their descendants spread northward, eventually reaching a point on the Missouri too dry for corn farming. From these corn farmers on the Missouri, near its confluence with the Knife River, came seasonal hunters who eventually stayed in Montana to become a mighty tribe, the Crow Indians.

At first, few hunters filtered into the area. Unlike their ancestors, these people stalked game that stampeded at the sight of humans. People relied upon roots, berries, rabbits and other small game, and occasional bison.

A smaller bison had replaced the extinct giant bison of prehistory. Early Indians sometimes drove large numbers of the beasts off cliffs like the Rimrocks. But such kills were too seldom to provide a reliable food supply.

A people called "Big Shield Warriors" by archaeologists adorned the Indian Caves south of the river with self-portraits. Ancestors of the modern Shoshone entered the area from the

Great Basin. Wandering in small bands, gathering and hunting, they left their mark on canyon walls.

The bow and arrow replaced the spear and throwing stick, but the success of the Native American bison hunters awaited the acquisition of Spanish horses about 1750.

The horse created a new life for people, who became wealthy with their easy access to bison meat and hides. Horses were the measure of a person's wealth, and a compelling reason for young men to raid the herds of other tribes. Horses provided a reason for war and a new mobility. Tribal conflicts intensified as white settlement pushed some tribes westward into the range of their ancient enemies.

The era of Plains Indians, who raided, counted coup and were romanticized in Western novels and movies, lasted barely 100 years. By 1850, whites had claimed most of the West. By 1876, a steady stream of military traffic used the wagon road up the Yellowstone Valley. By 1883 the bison had disappeared.

*Climbing to Pictograph Cave.*
BOB ZELLAR

*Yellowstone River near Park City, west of Billings.* LARRY MAYER

# The Yellowstone River

The Yellowstone River courses past Billings on a ramble from the Continental Divide toward a rendezvous with the Missouri River. The Yellowstone is more than Billings' water supply, more than a scenic amenity or historic transport route.

Nearly a third of Montana's population lives in the Yellowstone drainage. These Montanans are here because the river is here. Willard Fraser, flamboyant mayor of Billings and son-in-law of the poet Robert Frost, insisted that the boundaries of his city extended 300 miles in any direction because of the river: "We're here because it's there."

The Yellowstone River hasn't always been here. Roughly 80 million years ago, dinosaurs inhabited a sinking land in what is now Montana. The Mowry Sea, an extension of the Arctic Ocean, crept southward as the land settled. The Gulf of Mexico advanced northward. About 79 million years ago the two waters met and formed the Niobara Seaway, an inland sea that split the continent and sprawled between the present sites of Missoula and Chicago.

Time and ancient streams weathered a rugged mountain range to the west into rolling hills. Residues of that range formed massive sand bars and islands in the prehistoric sea. Sand in a layer 2,500 feet thick would become the Eagle Sandstone Formation, the strata Billings residents now call the Rimrocks.

*Geese on Lake Josephine at Riverfront Park.* BOB ZELLAR

Time passed and so did the dinosaurs, which disappeared about 65 million years ago. New mountains rose to replace the early range. Twenty to 30 million years ago an infant stream—the Yellowstone—carved through the sediment of the old inland ocean.

Roughly 1.5 million years ago, rain falling on prehistoric Montana coursed north in three major drainages: the Missouri, the Musselshell and the Yellowstone. Then, another change in the global weather system caused the polar icecap to thicken and spread, and a sea of ice crawled southward.

Snow fell on tundra and northern prairies. Snow fields still retreated under the assault of the summer sun, but each century the retreat grew shorter. White plains reflected sunlight back to the heavens. The atmosphere chilled and the ice advanced.

Plowing south, the continental glacier overran northern Montana and bulldozed riverbeds. The ice wall struck the Missouri River southeast of the Bearspaw Mountains, damming the flow and creating a glacial lake. The same icy mass collided with the Musselshell and the Yellowstone, which

formed more lakes. The ice sheet pushed the stubby rivers and their terminal lakes deep into present-day Montana, before a global warming trend around 18,000 years ago halted the ice advance.

Torrential rains lashed the earth for centuries. As the great ice mass receded, it left behind a great trough of rubble. Bloated by the rain pouring off the massive glacier, the Missouri's Glacial Lake Great Falls overflowed into the gap between the receding ice and the rubble. The trickle grew to a flood as the Missouri finally escaped its glacial impoundment.

The Missouri flowed eastward and joined the liberated Musselshell and Yellowstone rivers, to form the modern Missouri. In the middle of the continent the new waterway joined the Mississippi River and coursed south to the Gulf of Mexico.

Until the Ice Age's end, only animals such as giant bison, great cats, camels, and mammoths roamed the Yellowstone River Valley. The

first humans came overland when the retreat of the continental glacier opened an ice-free corridor from Alaska to Montana. Centuries later, the Crow Indians hunted and camped in this valley.

The La Verendrye brothers were once believed to be the first white explorers to reach this area. Francois and Joseph-Louis de La Verendrye, sons of French Canadian fur agent Pierre de La Verendrye, spent a winter (sometime between 1738 and 1743) in the Mandan villages, then pushed southwest. Historians today are not sure whether the La Verendryes reached the Big Horn Mountains of Wyoming or stopped at the Black Hills of South Dakota.

Charles Le Raye, another French Canadian, became the prime candidate for the honor of first white person to visit Montana after historians discarded the La Verendryes.

Captured by Indians, Le Raye was forced to travel through the region during the winter of 1802–1803. His party reached the Yellowstone—which they called the Jaune—

July 15, 1802. The group wintered with the Crows on the Stillwater River. Le Raye escaped the next spring with an account of his wanderings.

Fur trader Antoine Larocque published an account of his trip up the Yellowstone. On a September morning in 1805, in the vicinity of present-day Billings, he wrote:

"The current of this beautiful and great river is very great. The savages say there are not any falls there."

In 1806, Lewis and Clark crossed the Missouri–Yellowstone divide to the present site of Livingston. Captain William Clark found plenty of river but a lack of trees that were big enough to build canoes. The abundant western cottonwood could not fill the bill.

Clark and company hiked almost to the present site of Billings before finding prairie cottonwood, a much larger species. In several days of hiking the party saw just one Indian, but lost 50 horses to cunning Crow warriors.

Twenty years after the passage of Lewis and Clark, fur traders replaced dugout canoes with a bull boat that could carry three tons. Built of bison hide stretched over a frame 30 feet long by 12 feet wide, these improved boats

freighted furs to civilization for many years, until they were gradually replaced by flatboats or mackinaws.

Mackinaws were built of cottonwood planks, whipsawed from logs cut along the river. Though lacking sails and a mast, they resembled Viking ships. They were pointed at both ends and rose three feet above the waterline amidship. Many were 50 to 60 feet long with a 12-foot beam. Too bulky to be dragged upstream, the mackinaw was built for a single voyage. In St. Louis it was unloaded, dismantled and sold for lumber.

Days of the mountain men and fur traders were only memories when heavy traffic resumed on the Yellowstone in the 1860s. Gold miners from the western gulches found the Yellowstone River an easy way to return to the

United States, and escape from Montana winters.

A boat builder at Benson's Landing on the Big Bend sawed planks while the miners mucked for gold at Virginia City. Each fall, newspaper ads called for passengers and freight for the trip to the nearest railhead.

Hiking from Virginia City, their luggage in ox-drawn wagons, the miners embarked in bunches of 60 to 150. Prosperity loved company when the Sioux were harrying downstream stretches of the Yellowstone and Missouri.

The mackinaws carried 25 men apiece and were advertised to be bullet-proof. The fare was $25. The 1866 fleet made it to the railhead, but the Indians were unimpressed. The following year's flotilla was attacked near the mouth of the Big Horn River

*Ling fishing on the Yellowstone River east of Billings.* LARRY MAYER

and one man was killed. The pilot boat of a flotilla of 16 carrying 250 miners swamped and overturned at the mouth of the Clarks Fork River. The *St. Joseph Herald* reported $3,500 in gold lost in that wreck. The value of that dust today would exceed $500,000.

The confluence of the Clarks Fork and the Yellowstone remains a fine place to wreck a boat today. A set of standing waves at the junction teaches hotdog paddlers humility during the annual Peaks to Prairies Triathlon.

Between 1867 and 1873 river traffic dwindled to a trickle. Sioux pushed out of their traditional homelands into Crow country made the valley unhealthy for whites. As gold miners abandoned Virginia City for Helena, the downstream flow of people and gold dust shifted from the Yellowstone to the Missouri.

The steamboat evolved as rivermen probed the upper reaches of the Missouri. A steamboat christened *The Yellowstone*, built by Pierre Choteau of the American Fur Company, was the first to reach the mouth of the Yellowstone, in 1832. By the 1840s two steamboats churned the waters of the lower Missouri. Stoutly built with a shallow draft, these "mountain boats" filled a special chapter in the history of river boating's golden age.

That golden age would be as brief as that of the mountain men. Dawning in 1850 with the appearance of luxurious passenger steamers, it ended a decade later in the frenzy of railroad building.

In the early 1860s, plans to subdue the Sioux after a Minnesota massacre included an army post on the Yellowstone River. The Yellowstone became a military highway as General Alfred Sully marched against the Sioux in 1864 with the intent of building a fort on the Yellowstone. Eight steamers gathered in St. Louis that spring to supply the expedition. Grant Marsh, destined to be the greatest pilot and master on the Yellowstone, made his first trip to the upper Missouri as mate aboard the *Marcella*.

Sully's campaign failed to corral the Sioux, but the supply mission proved the Yellowstone navigable by shallow-draft steamers. Nearly a decade passed before steamboats returned to the river. Boiler smoke drifted down the river again in 1873. At the helm was none other than Captain Grant Marsh. Marsh joined the Coulson brothers, Martin and John, in forming the Coulson Packet. Of the company's seven boats, the *Far West* was Marsh's match. The captain and the steamer would make history together.

Designed for the upper Missouri and built in Pittsburgh at a cost of $24,000, the *Far West* stretched 190 feet from stern wheel to prow. With a 33-foot beam and a very small cabin, she carried 397 tons. Her compact superstructure offered little resistance to the winds that blow on the upper Missouri. In 1876, Marsh made his historic and heroic race from the mouth of the Big Horn River to Bismarck, carrying the wounded from the Little Bighorn battle.

The previous year, Marsh had proved his knowledge of the river's wiles in a boat christened the *Josephine*. Built to Marsh's specifications, she was a stern wheeler, with two engines and two boilers, 178 feet long and 31 feet across the beam, capable of carrying 300 tons. In 1875 the dauntless captain had pushed the *Josephine* upriver to a point estimated to be 250 miles above the Powder River, tying up at the present site of Riverfront Park southeast of Billings.

Marsh stopped more than

100 miles short of the river's source near Yount's Peak, on Two Oceans Pass in Wyoming. Here, a creek rooted in mountain snowmelt spills off both sides of the divide. A fish fighting its way up the Yellowstone could reach the Snake River, then the Columbia and eventually the Pacific Ocean.

In fact, Montana's cutthroat trout used precisely this path over the Continental Divide to the Yellowstone and as far downstream as the Tongue River.

The cutthroat's invasion was fairly recent in terms of geologic and evolutionary time. Genes of the native cutthroat have had little time to drift since the west slope cutthroat carried them over Two Oceans Pass into what is now Yellowstone National Park.

Yellowstone River lovers boast that their stream is "wet, wild and dam free." The Yellowstone is the longest free-flowing river in the contiguous 48 states. That status was once in doubt.

Montana is a state rich in resources. In the early 1970s, many Montanans were ready to sacrifice one treasure for the development of another. Schemes for damming (some say damning) the river at the Allen Spur notch above Livingston have been around since early in the century.

A weekly newspaper editor once asked:

"If the Yellowstone runs more than 9 million acre feet per year, what is the harm in catching the flood waters and using 3 or 4 million acre feet that would otherwise rush past us into North Dakota?"

It was a good question.

Not everyone was anxious to hear good answers.

Catching the flood—"surplus" water raging downstream—to green an arid Montana and feed a booming industry did present problems.

The first problem was the flooding of 31 miles of the Paradise Valley. Massive water consumption downstream would demand the construction of the long-debated Allen Spur Dam upstream. But more important to Yellowstone River fans was the certainty that the dam would damage the river along its entire run.

Regulated rivers settle into a single channel, soon lose their islands and eventually lose the woods and thickets girding them. An undammed river wanders in its valley, carving new channels and abandoning old ones. Brush and cottonwoods thrive on the islands and along the strand. These cottonwood and wild rose bottoms harbor an incredibly rich diversity of plant and animal life. In one 40-acre patch of river bottom (Billings' Two Moon Park), local Audubon members found more than 200 species of birds.

*Irrigation fields near Billings.*
LARRY MAYER

# The Natives

## The Crow Indians

*Crow sundance approximately 1930s.* PHOTOGRAPHER UNKNOWN; COURTESY OF MRS. HERTHA LYNCH, BILLINGS

Crow people called Billings' site: "Ammalapashkuua," or "place where we cut wood." This river bottom was a favorite camp, tucked between sandstone cliffs and the Yellowstone River, a salubrious spot of plentiful wood, water, and game.

At the height of the tribe's power, this camp was at the center of Crow Country. It may have been a seasonal bivouac of tribal ancestors, before there was a Crow tribe.

Corn, discovered somewhere in Mexico, had nourished a culture that spread northward to other tribes. Somewhere in the Eastern woodlands the ancestral

tribe of all Siouxian-speaking peoples became sedentary corn farmers. Driven by population pressure, one branch of this group spread up the Missouri to its confluence with the Knife River. There they lived in great villages of earthen lodges in what is now North Dakota. Beyond this point, climate made corn cultivation a gamble at best, but the river road beckoned the curious westward, into the valleys of the Yellowstone and Upper Missouri.

Around 1500 A.D., a scarcity of game may have driven a band of these farmers to abandon their fields and seek a new home in the rich bison country upstream. Crow legend tells of their split from the farming tribes of the upper Missouri. Crow historians say their people left the earthen lodges when two women quarreled over a bison paunch. Anthropologists speculate that a food shortage triggered the split. The same story appears in the legends of the Gros Ventre to explain their split from the Arapaho.

One legend tells of a wandering people who called themselves "Bidego" or "Our Side." Bidego would become the Apsaloka or "Children of the Big Beaked Bird." Other tribes described them in sign language with a flapping of arms, which whites mistakenly translated as "Crow."

It is likely that the earliest Crow people planted corn on the Missouri each spring,

rode off to the Yellowstone Valley for a summer bison hunt, and returned laden with jerked meat in time for the fall harvest. In time, the Crow probably quit farming altogether. They planted only small patches of sacred tobacco, and never farmed again until the coming of white people. The art of making pottery, and other sedentary crafts, were forgotten as they acquired new skills associated with the nomadic life.

Sometime in the first half of the 18th century, a party of Crow warriors quested south. Deep in the Southwest, the raiders struck a village and rode away with the Crow tribe's first horses. The acquisition destined the Crow to dominate a land as big as England and Wales combined. Without horses

**Above:** *Chief Plenty Coups of the Crow.* MONTANA HISTORICAL SOCIETY
**Top:** *Crow Fair dancers.* LARRY MAYER

***Above:*** *Medicine Deer Rock, a Northern Cheyenne vision quest site.* MICHAEL CRUMMETT
***Top:*** *Moonrise over Rosebud Hills, Northern Cheyenne Reservation.* MICHAEL CRUMMETT
***Right:*** *Mule deer.* JAMES WOODCOCK

existence on the high plains was precarious. With horses, the Crow harvested a wealth of bison meat, and enjoyed a mobility farmers could not afford.

The Crow continued to visit their cousins at the Mandan villages. More than a century later they abandoned their nomadic ways only after whites forced them onto a reservation.

European invaders brought more than guns and horses to change the course of Native America's history. Smallpox found its way up the Missouri to decimate the tribes of the High Plains. One of these epidemics swept a Crow village where Billings now stands. A young man returning with a hunting party learned that the disease had killed his sweetheart. Disconsolate, the teenager announced his intention to join his love in "the Other Side Camp." The young man's best friend said he too would go.

Mounting a single horse, the young men told an elderly woman to witness and remember their deed. The pair rode to their deaths aboard a white horse, plunging from a cliff at the edge of what is now the fairgrounds. The cliff, an unspectacular sandstone cutbank beneath a parking lot, is only about 60 feet high. Much of it was blasted away during the construction of MetraPark.

The romantic tale of young love lives on in Crow oral tradition, but has been distorted by whites. In the telling and retelling by non-Indians, two boys and one pony became scores of Indians to "appease the gods who sent the pox." The story's locale was switched from the bank behind Metra to the great sandstone cliffs of the majestic South Rims across the river.

Today, that great bluff is known locally as "Sacrifice Cliff."

Though history was twisted, the cliff was aptly named. It was one of a number of sites favored for vision quests. From these heights, Crow warriors, and boys who would be warriors, spent four days in meditation without food or water, seeking the dream that would guide their lives and help ensure the survival of their people.

Never a large tribe (8,000 before smallpox reduced their number to 1,000), the Crow saw themselves as "the mighty few." They held their land against formidable foes. To the north ranged the Blackfeet, a fierce and powerful people. To the east, the Crow were pressed by the great Sioux nation. Cheyenne and Arapaho held the land to the south. All of them coveted Crow Country.

Crow history is filled with tales of desperate stands against overwhelming numbers. Crow warriors repelled all challengers until the coming of those people too numerous to count—the whites.

French fur traders wandering into this region in 1742 found a race of *"beaux hommes"* living in a land of "shining mountains." The handsome men discovered by the La Verendrye brothers in their westward quest were Crow warriors.

Captain William Clark learned of this nation in 1804, shortly after reaching the Mandan villages on the upper Missouri. Clark noted that the Mandan and Sioux had the same word for water. He noted, too, that the Mandan, Gros Ventre and Crow spoke a similar language and were probably once members of the same tribe.

Crow Country was once a great triangle, with its apex in Wyoming's Wind River Mountains and its base the divide between the Missouri and Yellowstone rivers— more than 60,000 square miles. Passion for their land is reflected in the words of the great chief Arapooish:

"Crow Country is good country. The Great Spirit put it in exactly the right place. Whenever you are in it you fare well. Whenever you go out of it, whichever way you may travel, you fare worse.

"If you go south, you have to wander over great barren plains. The water is warm and bad, and you meet with fever and ague.

"To the north it is cold. Winters are long and bitter and there is no grass. You cannot keep horses there but must travel with dogs. What is a country without horses?

"On the Columbia they are poor and dirty, paddle about in canoes and eat fish. Their teeth are worn out. They are always taking fish bones out of their mouth. Fish is poor food.

"To the east they dwell in villages. They live well but they drink the muddy waters of the Missouri. That is bad. A Crow's dog would not drink such water.

"About the forks of the Missouri is a fine country—good water, good grass, plenty of bison. In summer it is almost as good as Crow Country but in winter it is cold, the grass is gone and there is no salt weed for the horses.

"Crow Country is exactly in the right place. It has snowy mountains and sunny plains, all kinds of climates and good things for every season. When the summer heat scorches the prairie, you can draw up under the mountains where the air is sweet and cool, the grass fresh and the bright streams come tumbling out of the snow banks. There you can hunt the elk, the deer and the antelope when their skins are fit for dressing. There you will find plenty of white [grizzly] bears and mountain sheep.

"In autumn, when your horses are fat and strong from the mountain pastures, you can go down onto the plains and hunt buffalo or even trap beaver on the streams.

"When winter comes on, you can take shelter in the woody bottoms along the rivers. There you will find buffalo meat for yourselves and cottonwood bark for your horses. Or, you may winter in the Wind River Valley where there is salt weed in abundance.

"Crow Country is exactly in the right place. Everything good is to be found there. There is no country like Crow Country."

The Crow Nation's sole contact with the Lewis and Clark Expedition proved a delight for the Indians and a nuisance for the whites. On the return trek to St. Louis, Captain William Clark lost 50 horses to the Crow.

The Crow may have charged Clark's party a hefty trespass fee paid in horses, but the tribe never waged war on whites. Casting their lot with the only force capable of checking the advance of the Sioux into Crow Country, Crow chiefs allied their warriors with the U.S. Army. Crow scouts fought with General George Crook at the Battle of the Rosebud. Crow scouts warned Lt. Col. George Armstrong Custer of Sioux strength on the Little Bighorn, and left his command before he led his men to annihilation.

The United States acknowledged its Indian ally's ownership of more than 35 million acres of Crow Country. But the same pressure of whites expanding westward that sparked war with the Sioux, prompted the government to wrest large chunks of land from the tribe.

Giving up the Stillwater and Boulder drainages and a large portion of the Yellowstone Valley, Crows struggled to survive in a changing world. Chief Plenty Coups set an example, building a two-story log home and opening a store. The great chief warned his people, "With an education you are whiteman's equal. Without it, you are his victim." The great chief's words live on.

*Right: Ali and Palmy Woodenlegs, Northern Cheyenne, ride a parade travois on the Fourth of July.* MICHAEL CRUMMETT
*Below: Pryor Mountains and Badlands.* RICK GRAETZ

*Facing page, top: Interior of a Lakota lodge.* MICHAEL CRUMMETT
*Bottom left: Northern Cheyenne eagle staff.* MICHAEL CRUMMETT
*Bottom right: Dallas Wallowing Bull at the Northern Cheyenne Pow Wow.* MICHAEL CRUMMETT

# The Northern Cheyenne Indians

*G*lory and tragedy color Cheyenne history. Often, the two are mixed.

Centuries ago, a group of Algonquin-speaking emigrants from the Eastern woodlands lived in earthen houses, and farmed corn on the Missouri. They called themselves the "Desert People" or "Plains People." A poor rendering of this name into Sioux produced "Shi-he-na" which evolved into "Cheyenne." At some point the tribe was enlarged by the addition of a band of distant cousins who called themselves the "Suhtai" or "The Descendants."

The tribe would split, re-unite, and split again before the Northern Cheyenne found sanctuary on the Tongue River east of the Crow Reservation.

Cheyenne legend and literature says Sweet Medicine spelled out the tribe's future long ago. A prophet and cultural hero, Sweet Medicine foretold the coming of the white people, the disappearance of the bison, and the bison's replacement by cattle. He comforted the Cheyenne with news of a great bounty—a round hoofed animal with a shaggy neck, the horse. Just before he died, Sweet Medicine left the Cheyenne with the grim prophecy of a time when they would forget their old ways, take up the ways of the whites, quarrel amongst themselves, and act crazy.

Modern Cheyenne leaders cite the Sweet Medicine stories as prophecy of today's political in-fighting, alcoholism, and drug abuse, all aggravated by poverty.

By 1650, the Plains horse culture was spreading, enlarged with stock captured from Spanish settlements in the Southwest. At about the time American colonists declared their independence from England, the acquisition of horses liberated the corn farmers of the upper Missouri and triggered that brief, bloody and romantic era of the Plains Indian bison hunters.

The Sioux and Cheyenne shared a portion of the Great Plains that stretched from Minnesota and Iowa into Montana and Wyoming. They raided their enemies, killed bison, and thrived for nearly a century.

Everything changed in the

mid-1800s. Guns disrupted the balance of power, exacerbated by the whites who supplied the arms.

By this time the Cheyenne tribe had split again. Bands that ranged farther south became the Southern Cheyenne. The Southern Cheyenne were victims of the infamous 1864 Sand Creek Massacre in Colorado. The Northern Cheyenne and their Sioux allies climaxed their fight against invasion with a victorious battle at the Little Bighorn.

The Bozeman Trail led across the Powder, Tongue and Big Horn rivers—prime bison grounds claimed by both Cheyenne and their Crow enemies. The Northern Cheyenne and Sioux were enraged that the Army guarded this trail that trespassed on their territory. In 1867, Sioux chief Red Cloud led his allies in a war that forced the Army to close the forts built to protect the trail.

In 1872, Northern Cheyenne and Sioux attacked a group of railroad surveyors and their army escort near the present site of Worden. In 1873 the surveyors returned with a much bigger military escort. The escort, commanded by General Alfred Sully, included a young Civil War hero, Lieutenant Colonel George Armstrong Custer.

The following year, Custer led a surveying expedition into the Black Hills of South Dakota. The hills were sacred to both Sioux and Cheyenne. It was at Bear Butte on the northern fringe of the Black Hills that Sweet Medicine had the vision of the future.

Custer's report of gold in the Black Hills loosed a flood of white prospectors into the area. The invasion of the hills made a mockery of the Fort Laramie Treaty of 1868. As settlers poured into the hills, bands of Northern Cheyenne and Sioux slipped away from the agencies to join non-treaty bands in the Powder River and Big Horn River country.

As collision of the two cultures became inevitable, President Ulysses S. Grant decided to ignore the white violation of the Black Hills, and force the "renegades" to return to the reservation. By 1876, the stage was set for the last great campaign of the Indian wars.

Three columns advanced on the Indian bands in Montana Territory. Custer led the swift Seventh Cavalry right into the Indian allies at the Little Bighorn. Troops led by Major Marcus Reno were pinned down on a small bluff overlooking the river. Captain Frederick Benteen arrived with his troops and ignored an order to ride to Custer's assistance. Before dusk, Custer and 260 men were dead.

Sioux chief Gall's warriors had met Custer's soldiers at Medicine Tail Coulee. Reel-ing backward, Custer's command was hit in the flank by a second force led by Northern Cheyenne chief Two Moon and Sioux chief Crazy Horse.

The Indians won the battle but had no chance of winning the war. The Army pursued the renegade bands into the winter. In November of 1876, soldiers caught Dull Knife's band at the head of Crazy Woman Creek. Soldiers and Pawnee scouts captured many Cheyenne horses and the band's winter food supply. When Dull Knife's Cheyenne people fled to join Crazy Horse's Sioux, the attackers burned lodges, blankets and robes.

Two Moon's band surrendered at Fort Keogh (Miles City) in early 1877. After wintering with the Sioux, Dull Knife surrendered in April.

Shortly after Dull Knife's surrender, most Northern Cheyenne were sent south to join the Southern Cheyenne in Oklahoma. It was a bitter move. Many Northern Cheyenne had visited relatives in the south, but few wanted to live there. Leaving a land where bison were still plentiful, they were driven to the southern Great Plains where heavy hunting had made game scarce. Forced to live on three-quarter rations, unaccustomed to the climate, and vulnerable to diseases seldom before encountered, Northern Cheyennes sickened and began to die.

**Top:** *Young competitor in the Eastern Montana College Pow Wow.* BOB ZELLAR

**Opposite:** *Index and Pilot peaks in the Beartooth Mountains.* JOHN REDDY

In the summer of 1878, chiefs begged the superintendent to allow them to lead their people back to the north. Refused permission, Little Wolf announced they would leave without it.

Indian police caught the fleeing Cheyenne a day and a night later. Ordered to return to the reservation, Little Wolf replied:

"Go back and tell them we are going home. We don't want any fighting. If the Army wants to fight us, they can. We are not going back."

The Army did want to fight. Thousands of troops attempted to stop the Northern Cheyenne exodus. Telegraph wires crackled with reports of Little Wolf's movements. Troop trains shuttled from one point to another. In spite of good communications and transportation, the Army was unable to check the Cheyennes' homeward flight. Fighting a series of battles and winning every one, the Cheyenne reached the north, where they split into two bands led by Dull Knife and Little Wolf.

Little Wolf's people wintered in the Sand Hills of Nebraska. Dull Knife was met by soldiers and persuaded to surrender. Confident that he was home, the chief voluntarily led his followers into Fort Robinson in northern Nebraska.

The band was told it would be sent back to Oklahoma. Feeling betrayed, Dull Knife's people barricaded themselves in the barracks where they had been staying. More than half of these people were killed in a futile attempt to escape. Most of the survivors were sent to the Pine Ridge Agency in South Dakota, where they lived with the Sioux until joining Little Wolf's people in Montana on land that eventually became the Northern Cheyenne Reservation.

# Pompeys Pillar

*P*ompeys Pillar towers above the Yellowstone River. It served as a rendezvous point for wandering peoples long before the first white people visited this valley.

In 1806 Captain William Clark scratched his name on the pillar's soft sandstone face, on his way home from the epic Lewis and Clark Expedition to the Pacific. That signature remains the only physical trace on the trail of an exploration as daring and probably more important than more recent flights to the moon.

Clark was not the first white to inscribe a name on this rock. French-Canadian trapper Francois Antoine Larocque had met Lewis and Clark at the Mandan villages and asked to accompany the expedition. A suspicious Lewis and Clark refused permission. Larocque struck out overland with several Indians, on a mission to gather furs and make contact with tribes in the region. He reached the pillar September 15, 1805, nearly a year ahead of Clark.

Larocque described the pillar as "a whitish perpendicular rock on which had been sketched with a red soil, a battle between three people on horseback and three others on foot."

More than a half century after Larocque read this bit of Indian history, James Stuart, Captain of the Yellowstone Expedition, noted "bison to be seen in every direction and very tame...a perfect paradise for a hunter."

Others who trailed by Pompeys Pillar would fill both a rogues gallery and a hall of fame.

Crow Chief Arapooish rode this way in pursuit of Cheyenne warriors who had struck a small village of his people, killing men, capturing women and children, and driving away horses.

Captain Clark had noted a large number of corrals on the islands on the bottom lands about Pompeys Pillar. These facilities would have been a welcome sight to

*Graffito by Captain William Clark on Pompeys Pillar.*

28

Arapooish and his men. Here they would have stopped to rest and replenish food supplies, for the Crow march was a long one. Arapooish caught the raiders on the Cheyenne River several hundred miles south of the Yellowstone. Crow accounts say his force killed 1,000 Cheyenne warriors and captured 1,000 prisoners and 1,000 horses. Exaggeration of the victor's report is a tradition, but no one exaggerated what happened on the trek back to the Yellowstone. Neither Crow nor Cheyenne won in the end. Smallpox killed nine of every ten persons, respecting neither victor nor vanquished.

Crow called the Pompeys Pillar camp "Ishbeeaashe" or "Mountain Lion Valley." Clark named it Pompeys Pillar in honor of the youngest member of the expedition, Baptiste, son of Sacagawea. Clark called the boy "my little Pomp," perhaps a Shoshone slang for Little Chief.

Baptiste was born at the Mandan villages while the Lewis and Clark Expedition wintered there in 1804. He was 18 months old when Clark's party reached the pillar.

The lives of Baptiste and his Shoshone mother have sparked lively histories and romantic legends. Authors of romantic novels portray Sacagawea as chief guide and savior of the Lewis and Clark Expedition. She was probably neither. She was, however-

er, an American heroine whose life story needs no embellishment.

Adventure stalked the Indian madonna, catching her for the first time on the banks of the Madison River in what is now western Montana. She was picking berries when a Hidatsa raider captured her and carried her off into slavery in what is now North Dakota.

She was sold, or perhaps lost in a gambling game, to a French Canadian named Toussaint Charbonneau.

Charbonneau joined the Lewis and Clark Expedition at the corn farming villages of the Mandan in the winter of 1804–1805. The explorers must have been pleased with the Frenchman's decision to bring his young Shoshone wife. The expedition would need horses from the Shoshones to cross the mountains.

Sacagawea was seldom mentioned in the Lewis and Clark journals. Two typewritten pages might contain all we know of her. Captain Clark recorded Sacagawea's death in the early 1820s. She would have been less than thirty years old.

Had it not been for writer Eva Emery Dye, Sacagawea might have been forgotten. Leader of a suffrage group, Dye was searching for a heroine when she discovered the Shoshone woman in the Lewis and Clark journals.

Dye later recalled, "Out of a few dry bones I found in the old tales of the trip, I cre-

ated Sacajawea and made her a living entity." Scores of Sacagawea tales were based on Dye's creation.

A second source of the legend is found not in books but in the person of an elderly Indian woman who was buried on the Wind River Reservation in 1884. There is no doubt this woman existed. But her claim to be Sacagawea and her assertion that her lazy and alcoholic son was Baptiste is more than dubious.

Who was the real Sacagawea? We know for certain that at age 16 she crossed an untamed continent with a baby on her back. Presence of the mother and child signaled peaceful intent to tribes along the way. That same presence made the mission not just a success but a triumph.

Did her wit and lore save the mission? Did she live to 100? Did she bring the Mandan sun dance to the Shoshones? Such questions are fuel for controversy we need not enter.

Others who made the great trek with Lewis and Clark were men of stamina, courage and resourcefulness. Sacagawea pulled her weight in this illustrious company, and won the admiration and affection of her peers. A century later, her example inspired women battling for equal rights. She became a pathfinder and spiritual mother of women pilots, doctors, and lawyers.

**Top:** *Pumpkin harvest at country garden, northeast of Billings.*  LARRY MAYER
**Left:** *At a mountain man rendezvous in Montana, visitors witness clothing and crafts from the era of Lewis and Clark.*  LARRY MAYER

**Facing page:** *Pompeys Pillar on the Yellowstone River east of Billings.*
JOHN REDDY

Sacagawea's son Jean Baptiste Charbonneau was born of mixed blood on the jagged edge of two cultures. He deserves his own chapter in the history of the West.

Baptiste was a toddler by the time the party reached Pompeys Pillar. When his parents left the expedition upon returning to the Mandan villages, Clark offered to raise the boy as his own. No doubt Clark promised to educate the child to prepare him for a place in a world of radical change. The baby's parents said the child was too young to leave his mother.

Later, his parents brought the boy to St. Louis. Clark's personal papers record payments to both a Catholic priest and a Baptist minister for the boy's education.

After being educated as Clark's ward in St. Louis, Baptiste traveled to Europe as the guest of Prince Paul of Württemberg. The personable Baptiste spent two years among the society of Old World royalty. He returned to the frontier to trap fur with the likes of Jim Bridger, the Robidoux Fur Brigade, and Kit Carson.

Pompeys Pillar became a familiar landmark for two other members of Clark's party: Nathaniel Pryor and John Colter.

Pryor may have been nursing a quiet rage when he arrived at this rock. Charged with pushing a herd of horses overland to the Mandan villages, Pryor had lost every one to Crow raiders.

John Colter, of Colter's Hell—now known as Yellowstone National Park—passed the pillar at least a half dozen times. Most of these times he was either hiking upriver, loaded with supplies and great expectations, or returning with a load of furs. The last time he passed this rock, he was naked, dirty, gaunt, and no doubt filled with despair.

Colter had begged for and received permission to leave the Lewis and Clark Expedition to join a pair of trappers bound upstream. He must have figured there was more for him in that great land than a voyager's pay and two years of grueling experience. He saw himself returning to St. Louis a rich man.

Colter, and the partners who furnished him traps in return for guide service, wintered somewhere in the Yellowstone drainage. Colter chose the Yellowstone over the Missouri to avoid conflict with the Blackfeet.

Colter's partners disappeared into the unrecorded mists of history. Colter might have followed them into that fog, but deep into the Dakotas on his way downstream with a load of fur in 1807 he met Manuel Lisa, a young Spaniard already established in the fur business.

In the winter of 1807 Colter struck out—with a 30-pound pack, ammunition and rifle—to contact Indians and urge them to bring furs to Lisa's fort at the confluence of the Big Horn and Yellowstone rivers. During this journey, Colter joined a band of Crow in a battle against Blackfeet warriors. Wounded in that conflict, he returned to the fort.

The next fall, Colter and a partner, John Potts—another Lewis and Clark veteran—hiked up the Yellowstone Valley, crossed the Bozeman Pass and trapped the headwaters of the Missouri.

Legend says that Colter and Potts were placing traps from a canoe when surprised by a party of Blackfeet. Potts was killed and Colter was stripped to the skin and given a head start in a race for his life. Plunging through sagebrush and cactus he outraced his captors to the Madison River five miles away. Hiding among some driftwood or inside a beaver lodge, Colter shivered until nightfall and slipped away into the darkness. Barefoot and naked, without food or fire, he recrossed Bozeman Pass and stumbled into Lisa's fort on the Big Horn eleven days later.

After two more scrapes with the Blackfeet, Colter returned to Fort Lisa with a younger partner, built a dugout and paddled 3,000 miles to St. Louis in 30 days.

During his wanderings in the West, Colter happened into the volcanic wonders of Yellowstone National Park.

A rugged crag overlooking the upper end of Yellowstone Lake is named for him.

If Pryor and Colter passed this pillar in a sour mood, one man arrived here in high spirits. Lieutenant Colonel George Armstrong Custer was part of an army escort to protect surveyors staking out a route for the Northern Pacific Railway.

Sioux invasion of Crow Country had delayed the 1872 railroad survey of valley. The work party was to survey from a point near the present site of Billings to the Powder River. The next year the survey returned with a large force. General D.S. Stanley commanded an expedition of twenty companies of infantry and most of Custer's Seventh Cavalry.

The 1873 expedition camped across the river from Pompeys Pillar. On August 15, Sioux scouts watched the party from the pillar, noting that a wash day had been declared and all hands were at the river. When the shore was covered with men, many of them bathing, the Indians opened fire.

Custer wrote, "The scampering of naked men up the hill was very comical." Only one man was injured.

Sioux harassed the surveyors from the beginning. Two skirmishes were fought near the present site of Forsyth. A full-scale battle 25 miles downstream from the pillar pitted Sioux against Custer's Seventh Cavalry in a dress rehearsal of a greater fight—the Battle of the Little Bighorn.

The battlefield in Yellowstone County where Custer met the Sioux and won, is unmarked and little known.

# Battle of the Little Bighorn

In late June of 1876, Lieutenant Colonel George Armstrong Custer and his Seventh Cavalry loped toward destiny, while Indian forces under Lakota chief Sitting Bull gathered on Lame Deer Creek. At the Little Bighorn River, these two larger-than-life warriors collided.

Cinematic reincarnations would distort the images of Custer and Sitting Bull. Each, in turn, would be remembered as hero and villain. Custer, mourned as a tragic hero in 1876, became the object of 20th century ridicule and the symbol of American genocide. Sitting Bull, perceived first as a blood-thirsty savage, evolved into today's notion of the noble Native American.

The stereotypes are not without a grain of truth, but even the best of them fit poorly. Sitting Bull and Custer were, if anything, worthy adversaries. In war's context—where a person is measured by the strength of the enemy—each makes a giant of the other.

Underlying the historic conflict was gold—the discovery in the Black Hills of Dakota Territory—in Sioux territory. A flood of white prospectors, settlers, and, finally, a railroad followed. In spite of treaties and promises, corralling the Plains Indians was central to this nation's plan for developing the West. Whites itched to reduce Indian holdings. Both politicians and frontier newspaper editors declared it was time for the Indians to become self-sufficient and give up their land.

Sitting Bull, who later declared himself "the last Indian," refused to submit to the captivity of reservation life. His charismatic leadership attracted thousands of others. The great campaign to return the Indians to their reservations found tens of thousands waiting for a showdown with the U.S. Army.

The stage was set. The Indian allies lacked only one ingredient of a victory that would fill the songs of the grandchildren of grandchildren yet unborn. The missing ingredient had nothing to do with men or munitions. Lacking was the medicine that would be glory's guarantee, a vision to set fighting spirits ablaze.

It was the quest of that medicine that filled Sitting Bull's dreams. He dreamed of towering sandstone streaked by lightning. The dream excited scouts. They had seen in daylight what the man had seen in dreams.

*Left: Battle of the Little Bighorn reenactment.* JAMES WOODCOCK

Elders found the great sandstone pillar protruding from a terrace above Lame Deer Creek. The lightning bolt, a bluish streak raking the tower's side, pierced the heart of a deer inscribed there by a wanderer from an earlier age.

The lightning bolt proved to be medicine's medicine. At the sun dance across the creek from the rock, Sitting Bull stared into eternity while the medicine men cut 150 pieces of flesh from his arms.

His vision was the medicine that made the recipe for victory complete. No mere to-ken or talisman—this was medicine to stop the sun, to seal the golden boy's fate, to make rivers race backward and the Little Bighorn run red with U.S. Government Issue blood.

White historians note that Sitting Bull was not among that hornet cloud of warriors boiling out of the valley of the Little Bighorn to meet Custer and his soon-to-be-dead Seventh. Custer buffs, smug admirers of the man come to slaughter women, children, and other "enemies of the United States," say the great chief cowered in his lodge while the battle raged.

Cowered indeed.

Sitting Bull had made his stand in the medicine lodge on Lame Deer Creek. He was tethered to the center pole by thongs attached to pegs embedded in his flesh, blood trickling from 150 wounds, like fringes of a buckskin shirt. He danced himself free of a body that fell in a swoon.

Unhindered by the freight of flesh, bone, and marrow, the great Lakota collided with the cosmos. Dancing in the electrical storm of prophecy, in a land where "maybe" becomes "shall be," in the glare of the Creator's presence, Sitting Bull received a vision to complete the victo-ry's prescription. He saw soldiers falling head first into camp.

Those who believe that grandfather spirits live in stones, that cedar smoke carries prayer to God, those who believe as Sitting Bull believed, know that the battle to come was already won. Sitting Bull sealed Custer's fate on the floor of the sun lodge.

While the Sioux leader sought his vision, Custer rode hard from the Tongue River toward the Little Bighorn.

Custer was a controversial leader. The West Point graduate had made his mark and earned a place in military history long before his rendezvous with death at the Little Bighorn. He had proved a careless student at the U.S. Military Academy. However, brilliance and courage in the field won him the temporary rank of general in the Civil War.

A badly beaten Union army had been cornered at Bull Run. Jeb Stuart's forces were galloping toward the Union's bloodied ranks to deliver the *coup de grace*. Unstopped, Stuart would have decimated the Union force. With a reckless and fearless abandon that marked his fighting style, Custer led his men in a attack that pierced Stuart's

*Above:* *After a grass fire swept through the battlefield site in 1985 archeologists recovered numerous artifacts. These are from the Reno-Benteen battle site.* LARRY MAYER

*General George Armstrong Custer.*
MONTANA HISTORICAL SOCIETY

flank and checked the Confederate attack.

A commander who *led* rather than *sent* his men into battle, Custer had more than a dozen horses shot from under him. His brother Tom held the Congressional Medal of Honor. Together, they purported to fear nothing.

Custer's pluck on the battlefield served him poorly in peace-time politics. Brash and headstrong, he was in trouble with his superiors. At a public hearing in 1876, he offended President Ulysses S. Grant by condemning the War Department's Indian policy and the frauds connected with it. Only the pressure of favorable public opinion enabled him to take part in the expedition organized against the Sioux.

The expedition left Fort Abraham Lincoln, North Dakota, in May 1876 under General Alfred H. Terry. It was directed against the forces assembled in Montana by Sioux chiefs Crazy Horse and Sitting Bull. On June 24, scouts reported an Indian village in a bend in the Little Bighorn River. Terry sent Custer with 600 men to bar the Indians' escape.

The next morning, Custer, fearing that the Indian camp might dissolve and that the enemy might melt into the vastness of the Great Plains, decided to disregard his orders. He sent a detachment under Captain Frederick Benteen to explore the area south of the riverbend. Soon afterward, Custer sighted the village. He then sent a column under Major Marcus A. Reno to approach the Indian camp along the river's west bank.

Fear that the Indians might escape was legitimate. The strike-and-run tactics of guerrilla warfare had served Indians well in war against lumbering armies trained and equipped to fight pitched battles.

The allied Indian force on the Little Bighorn numbered 6,000. The Army was misinformed about the size of their adversary; federal Indian agents had under-reported the number of Sioux slipping away from reservations.

Probably more important than Indian numbers was Indian élan fired by Sitting Bull's vision of soldiers falling into camp. Unknown to Custer, a recent Sioux victory over General Crook on the Rosebud demonstrated the vulnerability of white soldiers meeting a superior Indian force. The victory sparked zealous faith in Sitting Bull's medicine.

Custer's plan was simple and battle-tested. He would divide his force in two. One body would strike the enemy upstream, the other would cut the village in half. In more than a dozen earlier fights in the U.S. Army's campaign against the Plains Indians, this strategy had

*Sitting Bull, Lakota Sioux/Unkpapa medicine man.* DAVID F. BARRY PHOTO, WESTERN HISTORY DEPT., DENVER PUBLIC LIBRARY

sparked chaos in attacked villages.

With the village paralyzed by confusion and panic, an organized cavalry would scatter and kill warriors while capturing and destroying lodges, ponies and food supplies. Stripped of food, shelter, and the means to fight or hunt, the villagers would surrender, or limp back to the reservations.

That was the way it was supposed to work. Instead, Custer's defeat in the rolling hills along the Little Bighorn at Medicine Tail Coulee became one of the most famous battlefields in the world. The Battle of the Little Bighorn ranks with Napoleon's fall at Waterloo, the Battle of Bosworth Field, and the Battle of the Bulge as one of the most written-about fights in history.

What happened? Theories by the score have advocates numbering in the thousands, but the question lingers. Every explanation has its champions and detractors. Many blame Custer's vanity, believing that his arrogance and unwillingness to share the glory he thought would be his pressed him to attack without waiting for help from Terry or Gibbon. Others say a poor estimate of the Sioux and Cheyenne numbers prompted bad decisions on the battlefield.

In any case, it would seem likely that Custer died early in the fight. The straggling scatter of Seventh Cavalry corpses testifies to a rout, rather than the organized retreat Custer might have commanded.

Some historians believe Custer's fatal mistake was in trusting Major Reno to execute his part of the attack. Reno struck the village at its upstream end, catching the Indians (by their own report) by surprise. When Sioux warriors rallied to protect their women and children, Reno ordered his men to dismount and form a skirmish line across the valley. Drawing heavy fire, Reno fell back to the river and woods along the strand. Finally, he led his men in a headlong rush toward the high ground. This unexpected rout of the attackers freed the Sioux defenders to rush downstream toward the dust of Custer's attack.

Warriors boiled out of Medicine Tail Coulee like wasps from a hive. Unable to penetrate the valley camp, Custer's men were driven toward higher ground, overlooking the lower end of the village.

At the top of the ridge, troops staggering backward under Gall's attack collided with the assault led by Crazy Horse and Two Moon. Atop monument hill, the Sioux-Cheyenne assault closed on the Seventh Cavalry like the wings of a mousing hawk.

Two days later Crow scout Curley carried the battle news to the steamboat *Far West.* Army survivors suffering from heat, thirst, and bullet wounds were carried in litters, which were slung between mules, to the waiting steamer.

*Above:* Aerial view of the Battle of the Little Bighorn site. In the foreground is the area of the Indian encampment, top center is where Custer made his stand.
LARRY MAYER

**Right:** *Southwest of Billings.*
RICK GRAETZ

# Pryor Mountains

*T*he Pryor Mountains were born in the soup of a primeval sea. Here, antiquity lingers on mystic heights and lurks in hidden canyons.

The Pryors' foundation began when billions of shellfish, multiplied by millions of years, lived, died and left behind their shells in limestone strata hundreds of feet thick. When the ancient sea retreated, a grumbling within the earth thrust up great blocks of the white stone. These blocks, tilted upward from west to east, form the Pryors.

Elements and ages worked their wonders on the Pryors' ivory bones. Rain and snowmelt seeped through the limestone pores, dissolving soft rock and creating a maze of caverns and canyons.

Many caves became caches of hidden treasure. Bell Trap Cave captured and preserved the bones of prehistoric beasts including camels, giant cats, and bison. Some, like Big and Little Ice Caves, harbor small glaciers. Many served as transient homes to ancient peoples who left cryptic messages carved or painted on cave walls. Sinkholes betray the existence of scores of unnamed, undiscovered caverns.

While subsurface water sculpted caves and moved on to escape from distant springs, surface water chiseled the Pryors' canyons. Racing down from its source high in the Absaroka Mountains to the west, the Big Horn River sliced through a natural fault between the great mountain blocks. As the mountains rose, the river held its place. Today the river serves as a marker between the Big Horn and Pryor mountain ranges, and the exposed strata in its canyon reveal geologic history.

Yellowtail Dam is a soaring structure blocking the mouth of the canyon. The dam created Big Horn Lake, a favorite spot of anglers and recreational boaters. Impounding the once roily Big Horn transformed it into one of the nation's greatest blue-ribbon trout fisheries.

In its youth the Big Horn River paralleled a sister stream, the Shoshone River, in its race to the Yellowstone. While the Big Horn tumbled through a mountain canyon, the Shoshone's whitewater splashed through a passage now called Pryor Gap, and struck the Yellowstone a dozen miles downstream from the present site of Billings.

Millions of years ago, wind

*Crooked Creek Canyon, Pryor Mountains.* JOHN REDDY

and water nibbled the head-wall of a creek feeding the Big Horn River. It took eons to dissolve the headwall that divided the Shoshone and the Big Horn river drainages, but once the barrier was broken the creek captured the flow of the Shoshone River. Coursing down the creek bed, the Shoshone suddenly became a tributary of the Big Horn.

Pryor Gap was minus a river. Without the scouring water, sediment began to fill the canyon that was once 900 feet deeper than it is today. This dry canyon became the gateway to lands beyond the mountains. Ancient people, the first Indians to stream southward from the land bridge joining America and Asia, passed this way. Later, Plains Indians marked this pass with piles of stone that still can be seen today. John Colter found this crack in the mountains in his journey to the volcanic marvels of what would become Yellowstone National Park.

Another of the Pryors' canyons has an interesting past. Crooked Creek is a stream born in the braided silver threads of several great mountain springs near Big Ice Cave. The creek disappears into the hidden recesses of Crooked Creek Canyon. Narrow and deep, Crooked Creek Canyon can be viewed from either the Wild Horse Range or a road that follows much of the canyon's lip.

Few humans, white or red, have clambered over the barricades of boulders and brush to explore this canyon. For much of the way, the creek runs wall to wall. The 20-mile trek offers a wet and arduous challenge to wilderness veterans.

Paleolithic hunters known to anthropologists as "sheep eaters" were probably the first to probe this magnificent crevice. Ancestors of today's Shoshone Indians, these invaders from the Great Basin circulated between the Pryors and neighboring ranges, trapping bighorn sheep and foraging into the lowlands for seasonal hunts and harvests. Centuries later, Crow invaders drove these hunter–gatherers from the Pryors.

The great Crow chief Plenty Coups made his home on the cold creek spilling from the mouth of the Gap, and wandered down the valley carved by the ancient Shoshone River. Crow warriors defended their tribe against the Sioux, Blackfeet, and Gros Ventres in epic battles along Pryor Creek, in the Gap, and in the mountains above.

Three towers of limestone capped by bunchgrass, rabbit brush, and fir trees, overlook the reservation hamlet named for the mountains. The Crow say these Pryor outcroppings, dubbed "the Castles," are home to the Little People. Crows passing through the Gap often leave food, money, cloth or tobacco offerings at a rock cairn at the base of a cliff called Strikes the Arrow Rock.

Little People, Crow elders say, are a mystic and powerful race. Some of the area's most powerful healers had Little People as their spirit helpers. Crow oral history records the failure of a railroad that punched a tunnel through the rock beneath one of the castles. It is said that Little People broke the back of that ill-fated line.

Crow call these mountains "Baahpuuo." The modern name was left by a white man who never set foot in the Pryors. Captain William Clark reached the upper Yellowstone Valley in 1806 on his return to St. Louis. Clark intended to build canoes and float to a rendezvous with his partner, Captain Meriwether Lewis, on the Missouri River. He would send his 50 horses overland to the Mandan villages with Sergeant Nathaniel Pryor, one of the most trustworthy and resourceful men of the Lewis and Clark Expedition.

Clark and his men marched nearly to the present site of Billings before finding trees big enough to build dugout canoes. One night during this hike, Crow raiders stole half the horse herd.

Pryor struck out with the remuda's remaining animals in a frustrating drive toward the middle Missouri. He soon returned to the Yellowstone to catch the Clark dugout flotilla and ask for help. The horses, acquired from the Shoshone in western Montana, were trained to hunt bison. They bolted in pursuit each time drovers encountered a herd of the great beasts. Pryor pressed on with an extra man to ride point and drive away the bison.

Crow warriors struck again, leaving Pryor and his men on foot. The whites followed the horse trail for five miles before deciding the chase was hopeless. Walking back to the Yellowstone River, Pryor's party killed two bison and built bull boats to float downriver in pursuit of Clark.

Clark named a stream for his intrepid-but-frustrated sergeant. The mountains would share the name with the creek. If Pryor ever saw the mountains named for him, it was from the top of Pompeys Pillar where he launched his bull boats.

White settlers flooding the area early in this century scratched out a hardscrabble living on the flats skirting the Pryors. Others cut timber, raised cattle or prospected in the mountains.

The last white–Indian battle in this region was a rancher's ambush of several Crow cowboys in the Gap. A group of young Crows had found a lucrative opportunity in gathering horses off-reservation and driving them through the Gap, where they were held for ransom. Tired of paying the trespass fee, the rancher enlisted the aid of a friend and his hired man. Hiding among the brush and boulders, the trio opened fire on the raiders, killing two Crow riders and wounding a third.

Today, wild horses are the Pryors' crown jewels. Great stallions with ragged manes move their harems from the heights of the Dry Head Overlook to the canyons scarring the Pryors' flanks. The herd is a blend of mustangs descended from Spanish barbs, ranch animals that strayed, and farm horses abandoned by homesteaders starved out in the 1930s. Ranging in color from midnight black to sorrel to blueberry roan, wild horses of the Pryors remind us of a freedom once known by both humans and beasts.

# Bull Mountains

*F*ifty million years ago a swamp not unlike Louisiana's Atchafalia sprawled south of Billings. Cattails and horsetails flourished in the shallows, bay and sycamore trees studded the hummocks. Through the eons of that balmier era, plants and animals lived and died in the blackwater swamp and accumulated in the muck. They were compressed by their own weight into the veins of coal that now lace the strata of the Bull Mountains.

When erosion exposed one of these beds to lightning, the long-smoldering underground fire melted aluminum-rich kaolin clays into a ceramic mass. Native Americans would later chip tools from this natural china.

This crimson rock gives Dunn Mountain—referred to as the Red Buttes in 1876—its reddish cast.

In 1805, Captain William

**Bottom:** *Bull Mountains rancher Steve Charter drives his cattle to new pasture.* LARRY MAYER
**Top:** *In the Bull Mountains.* RICK GRAETZ

**Facing page:** *Bighorn Canyon at sunrise. Pryor Mountains in background.* LARRY MAYER

Clark officially named this range the "Wolf Mountains." Like many of the Lewis and Clark Expedition's names, this one did not stick.

Local legend and many histories claim that discovery of one of the last, lonely bull bison here gave the Bull Mountains their name. This story was set in type (if not carved in stone) by Mark Herbert Brown in his otherwise excellent history, *Plainsmen of the Yellowstone*.

In fact, trappers, traders and other white people recorded the name Bull Mountains long before the great herds vanished. The name no doubt came from the Crow Indians. The Bulls were an excellent wintering spot for both humans and beasts, providing refuge when the Arctic gave the north wind fangs. The name may be a reference to an abundance of bison, or to the humped shape of Dunn Mountain. A small range lacking cloud-busting peaks, the Bulls are called the Bull *"Hills"* by most Musselshell County residents.

Early hunters found an abundance of game, and shelter from both summer's heat and winter's fury. Clovis Paleo-Indians, fashioners of fine projectile points, hunted these coulees, ridges, and canyons 11,000 years ago.

In the late 1870s and early 1880s cattle driven north from Texas filled the Musselshell Valley north of the Bulls. In that same period, steamboats carried off the hides of hundreds of thousands of bison killed on the south side. With the bison gone, cattle here, and the railroad on its way, white people were firmly in control of the range that had fed and sheltered Indians for centuries.

In 1881, the Northern Pacific Railway began mining coal at the head of Railroad Creek. Probing the bones of the ancient swamp, Northern Pacific miners dug fossil fuel for the locomotives.

Early coal development in the Bulls was abandoned when the Northern Pacific turned to Carbon County mines for fuel. When the Milwaukee Railroad laid track north of the Bulls, mining boomed again and turned the cow town of Roundup into a coal town. Roundup, Kline and several smaller mine-mouth communities drew a rich mix of European immigrants. The rail industry's switch from coal to diesel crippled Roundup and other mining communities.

Sometime during this era, a group of Indians slipped away from their reservation and built a sun dance lodge near a spring at the foot of the Bulls. Secret sun dances in a time when government agents suppressed all traditional practices were not uncommon. But this one was different. Poles that formed the walls and supported the roof sprouted leaves and sent down roots after the dancers returned to their homes. This circle of cottonwoods continues to thrive, just off Highway 87, halfway between Billings and Roundup.

Native Americans hold the site to be sacred. Both Crow and Gros Ventre claim the living lodge. Members of these and other tribes sometimes stop to pray or hold pipe ceremonies in this grove, leaving behind bright cloth prayer flags and strings of tiny tobacco bundles.

Settlers filled the Bulls in the homestead era. They cut timber for cabins, built sawmills, carved roads, mined coal, and plowed and planted on ridgetops and creek bottoms.

A wave of bank failures swept Montana in the late 1920s. In prairie states, tales of the Dirty Thirties and the Great Depression feature the drought. Drought and rock-

bottom commodity prices bankrupted homesteaders, crushing the hopes they had for this new land. The settlers disappeared.

Many simply left. Turning their livestock loose, they loaded their families in wagons and drove away. Banks foreclosed on others. Most small holdings were swallowed by larger ranches.

Drought so severe that it killed trees sat heavy on the land. Insect infestations and disease spread through the Bulls' timber. Wildfire raced through infected stands of pine.

Fortunately, hard times didn't last forever. When the rains returned, native grass-

es returned to lands broken by the sodbusters, crowding out thistles, cheatgrass and other hardy denizens of the drought.

The one species never to return was the small farm-ranch operator. Families on every half-section were a thing of the past. Or so it seemed. In the 1960s a new breed of settler found the Bulls. A hunger for country air and tranquillity created a market for small tracts. Newcomers living on the land (but not off the land) were mostly retirees, or commuters with jobs in Billings. The land rush peaked in the 1970s when real estate developers carved sev-

eral large ranches into small acreages. Some of this wave of new settlers were driven from the Bulls in the 1980s when the Fox Creek Fire destroyed 50 homes.

The Bulls retain the scars of mining, logging and sodbusting. Today, the Bulls are a haven for wildlife, including pronghorns, deer, and wild turkeys. Red crossbills, mountain bluebirds, and lazuli buntings add a dash of color to the pines and grasslands of the Bulls. In season, male sage grouse and sharptail grouse dance at their leks, each hoping to lure a mate from among the hens that gather to watch.

**Left:** *Enjoying early autumn on Blue Creek Road south of Billings.* BOB ZELLAR
**Below:** *Lightning strikes a tree in Coulson Park, erstwhile site of the would-be city of Coulson.* LARRY MAYER

***Facing page:*** *Beartooth Pass.*
JOHN REDDY

# Coulson

*Coulson didn't miss by much! In the background, far beyond the freight wagons, can be seen Coulson on the right, and the east end of Billings on the left.* MONTANA HISTORICAL SOCIETY

Coulson winked into existence in 1887, when a group of Bozeman investors built a sawmill a couple miles east of what is now downtown Billings. Perry McAdow's livery stable, a ferry across the river, and John Alderson's hotel formed the nucleus of the new community. Within five years the town's promising future would be all in the past.

The speculators' timing was superb. The Army had driven the hostile Sioux from the Yellowstone Valley. Con-

gress would soon wrest ownership of the valley from the friendly Crow tribe. The Industrial Revolution's demand for machine-belt leather was contributing to the extermination of bison. Cattle from overstocked Texas ranges were trailing north to Montana grass. Finally, the railroad—that iron link to Eastern markets and potential settlers—was on its way.

The location of the new town was also excellent. Halfway between Seattle and Minneapolis, it lay across the river from the Crow Reservation and along the trail from Fort Custer to the cattle country farther north.

Newspaper and magazine writers have speculated that Coulson failed because it was too wild and woolly, or because its owners were too greedy. In fact, Coulson failed for the same reason many speculative real estate developments fail today: the owners did not have the power to make things happen.

Coulson died because it did not belong to Frederick Billings and Herman Clark, respectively president and chief engineer of the Northern Pacific Railway. The federal government had granted the railroad company millions of acres as an incentive to build. Clark and Billings, who recognized the potential of a new town at the line's midpoint, used their positions with the company to buy personally two sections of Northern Pacific land just upriver from Coulson. With the power of the railroad and the U.S. government behind them, Billings and Clark made their fortunes.

Before 1882, few Coulson residents dreamed their town was doomed. In fact, the town grew steadily. Alderson's hotel was the home of a stage station and post office. David Currier built a saloon. Trail hands whooped it up in Coulson while bootleg-gers ran whiskey to Indians across the river. Coulson's muddy streets thronged with cattle buyers, saddle tramps, prospectors lured by rumors of gold on the upper Yellowstone, bison hunters, railroad surveyors, soldiers, and the army of civilians (farmers, freighters, guides, scouts and others) serving the military in this area at the close of the Indian wars. Coulson's bustle drew preachers, gamblers, prostitutes, and midwestern business people ready to invest their life savings.

In 1877, Chief Joseph's Nez Perce killed two hunter-trappers on Joseph Cochrane's ranch near Coulson; burned Cochrane's tent house; and, according to some reports, torched the Coulson saloon.

Telegraph lines snaking across the prairie linked the town with the rest of civilization in 1878. In 1879 livery stable owner McAdow opened a general store. In the spring of that same year, belief in Coulson's prospects were strong enough to provoke a gunfight between two of its most prominent citizens. Hotel operator Alderson learned that saloonkeeper Currier intended to apply for a title to the townsite. Alderson rode all night to Bozeman to file his claim first.

After being outmaneuvered, Currier swore re-venge. He found Alderson at work on an ice house. Mrs. Alderson slipped her husband a rifle and he shot the armed saloonkeeper dead. A jury in Junction—another doomed Yellowstone County river town—ruled the shooting "justifiable homicide."

Approach of the railroad in 1881 spurred Coulson's growth. Convinced that the town would become the second Denver, builders and investors poured into town. Alderson platted the town, laying out three long avenues: River, Alba and Main.

The Bozeman *Avant-Courier* reported in February of 1882: "Coulson is one of the liveliest towns in Montana and building opportunities are only limited by the amount of materials obtainable. McAdow's Mill, having been run during the last few months to its fullest extent on railroad contracts, lumber for building purposes has been quite scarce, which has necessitated calling into requisition logs, slabs and every available thing which could possibly be worked into temporary structures. Other mills, however are being erected on Canyon Creek, and soon will measurably supply the demand for lumber."

Tent buildings bloomed on Main Street. Stores, saloons and dance halls flourished under canvas. A.K. Yerkes ran the *Coulson Post* newspaper from a slab building that had a dirt floor and dirt roof. Yerkes shared a room in the back of McAdow's store with Muggins Taylor during the winter of 1881-82. Taylor had been a civilian scout for the Army and had carried the news of Custer's defeat to the nearest telegraph at Fort Ellis above Bozeman. Taylor survived the Indian wars to become a deputy at Coulson, where he was fatally wounded by Henry Lumph, drunken husband of the town's laundress.

Another Coulson lawman, the legendary mountain man "Liver Eating" Johnson, was once asked by the sheriff in Miles City why he made so few arrests. Johnson said he had no jail for prisoners, so he "whomped" the bad guys and turned them loose.

Although Coulson lacked lumber and a lockup, it was booming nevertheless. In February of 1882 the *Post* ran an ad urging investors to catch on before the big boom of Coulson reached its height, and buy a lot on easy terms from John Alderson.

With a bakery, school, a wagon delivering ice, three general stores, a brewery, hotel, and five saloons, Coulson seemed on its way to greatness.

The "Big Boom" fizzled that summer. In the first week of April Coulson resi-

*Windmill west of Billings toward Molt.* RICK GRAETZ

dents learned that the railroad would stop a short distance upstream. The *Post* reported:

THE CITY LOCATED

THE RAILROAD DECIDES TO HAVE IT HERE

400 LOTS SOLD IN THE TOWNSITE PROPERTY JOINING COULSON

At first, publisher Yerkes tried to put the best face on the railroad's disappointing decision to bypass Coulson. The two towns, he wrote, are "really one, as they join each other [and] are upon a threshold of a future that is rich in promises."

Already, Yerkes was coppering his bets. The *Post*'s April 15 masthead read "Billings and Coulson." By June 10, Yerkes had joined other Coulson businesses in an exodus to Billings. Coulson was dropped from the *Post*'s masthead. Coulson's post office closed in August. By late summer, ads for the Coulson Brewery listed its address as East Billings.

While both money and new immigrants attended the birth of Billings, the

"Magic City," Coulson became the place to raise cane in the spring 1882. The same April 1 edition of the *Post* that reported a wind storm ripping through the dying town, also reported the shooting of a popular young waiter named Frank Redman, by a gambler named "Dutch Charlie."

Coulson founder Perry McAdow tried to keep the town alive with a horse-drawn railway between Coulson and Billings. Tickets stubs were good for two free beers at the Brewery. But not even free beer could save Coulson. Though the brewery continued to operate and a few people continued to live there, the *Billings Herald* exaggerated only a little when it reported in 1883:

"The Northern Pacific Railroad crosses the Yellowstone about one and a half miles east of Billings near the old town of Coulson, which is now uninhabited and desolate."

# THE MAGIC CITY

by Katherine A. Shandera

LARRY MAYER

# Frontier Town

*The first newspaper office in Billings. Publishers Edward A. Bromley and Alexander Devine put out their premier issue on June 1, 1882.* COURTESY PARMLY BILLINGS LIBRARY

*O*n August 22, 1882, the ground shook as a new creature charged across the alkali flats of Clark's Bottom. Its massive snout blew smoke and steam high into the sky, and its fierce, possessive scream reverberated off the rimrocks. Ignoring hopeful little Coulson, the creature rushed down the valley to its own infant town—Billings— sprawled in the dust, kicking and hollering for joy at the first sight of its mechanical mother.

The Northern Pacific Railroad had arrived at last. Billings residents staged a grand jubilee to celebrate the fact that their new town was now connected to the rest of the world by two strong iron bands. The frenetic activities churned up a cloud of alkali dust that coated everything, but nothing could dull the enthusiasm of the people of Billings.

Billings' conception back in October 1881 had been a rather stodgy affair, involving legal papers filed in Minnesota by the newly-formed Minnesota and Montana Land and Improvement Company. From that moment on, however, the embryonic town took on a boisterous life of its own.

News of the new community traveled quickly, and hundreds of settlers headed for Billings almost before the ink was dry on the platting map. In the spring of 1882, new residents were arriving daily by foot, horseback, and wagon train. Five thousand lots were purchased during the first month of sales. The newcomers threw up tents and shacks to live in, and gaily engaged in the business of building a town from the ground up.

Enterprise was the order of the day. A bakery, hotel, hardware store and millinery shop quickly appeared, along with saloons and dance halls. By early June, at least three doctors, two dentists and three lawyers were on the scene. Billings' first bank opened it doors, and a brewery was under construction. The recently founded *Coulson Post* moved its presses to Billings to become the *Billings–Coulson Post*, and go head-to-head against the even newer *Billings Herald*.

The town's growth was so chaotic that Herman Clark, manager for the Minnesota and Montana Land and Improvement Company, issued an order demanding the removal of "all shacks and tents located in the thoroughfares." Gradually, lumber, stone and brick building materials became available, and by August 1882, 124 houses were standing. In September, General James Brisbin wrote to a Chicago newspaper and called Billings the "Magic City" because of its incredible growth.

While all this hoopla was energizing the budding prairie town of Billings, the entire nation was also in the throes of excitement and change. New frontiers were being opened and daily life itself was undergoing profound changes. In 1870, there were no such things as electric lights or telephones. By 1900, forty percent of the nation would have electric service and one and a half million telephones would be in use. Bicycles and streetcars first enjoyed widespread popularity during the late 1880s, as did cameras and photography. Horses, as essential to daily life then as the internal combustion engine is today, were about to be replaced by that very engine.

Following the Civil War, building railroads was a national adventure in progress and power, akin to putting astronauts on the moon. In 1869, the first transcontinental tracks were completed, and people could travel from one coast to another in seven days rather than the six months previously required by boat. Coast-to-coast railways changed the face of the nation by opening the country's interior to development. Even time had to bend to the power of the rails. In 1883, the Department of Transportation facilitated train scheduling by instituting standardized time zones across the United States.

As exciting as this adventure was, the railroads weren't laying track for fun. They were in the business of making money, and to make money they needed the assistance and protection of the federal government. The government had its own purposes. In 1879, the Northern Pacific Railroad's money-making plans to build a transcontinental railroad through the northern territories meshed with the government's needs.

*Left:* Atop the rims, the grave of Luther "Yellowstone" Kelly, who scouted for Colonel Nelson Miles in the 1870s. BOB ZELLAR
*Below:* Historic district of Billings. LARRY MAYER

*Facing page:* Billings seen from the west, looking toward downtown. RICK GRAETZ

Montana was rich with gold, silver, and copper—powerful incentives for government cooperation with the Northern Pacific in building a railroad through the area. There was also a military incentive. Even though the American Indian wars were over, Indians continued to roam freely throughout the northwestern plains.

In order to strengthen its grip on the region, the government approved a route for the Northern Pacific that formed a supply line to 4,500 soldiers stationed along a series of frontier posts. The Northern Pacific was glad to oblige. U.S. troops were needed to protect construction workers from Indian attacks as the tracks began to be laid west of the Missouri River in 1879.

The tremendous expense of building a railroad through the wilderness was financed through federal land grants. For every 25 miles of track built in the territories, the Northern Pacific received alternating sections of land in an 80-mile-wide band along the tracks. To make a profit and finance more miles of track, the railroad needed to

sell land quickly and steadily to settlers, who would then use the railroad to ship supplies in and commodities out. The sale and development of land along the railroad's route was a golden opportunity for developers with a keen understanding of land transactions, and the right connections.

In early 1882, the Northern Pacific sold a large chunk of land to just such a group. The Minnesota and Montana Land and Improvement Company (MMLI) bought nearly 30,000 acres in the Clark's Fork Bottom of the Yellowstone River Valley. The MMLI was made up of current and former Northern Pacific officials, including past president Frederick Billings. Billings was a shrewd, nationally-respected businessman who had made his fortune as a land lawyer in San Francisco.

The company's purchase of the Clark's Fork Bottom land put MMLI in control of two squarely abutting sections on either side of the railroad right of way. It was an ideal situation for the company's real estate venture, a new town named Billings. Like all railroad towns, the original streets of Billings were laid out parallel to the railroad tracks. MMLI named the first street on the north side of the tracks Montana Avenue and the first street on the south Minnesota Avenue.

The depot was located on Montana Avenue, putting passenger arrivals and departures on the north side of the tracks. That decision made the south side of the tracks slightly less desirable, a distinction that remains today—far outlasting the reason behind it.

The influence, prestige and financial clout of the Montana and Minnesota Land and Improvement Company completely overshadowed Coulson's efforts to be adopted by the Northern Pacific. Billings was the favored one. It would grow strong and cocky under the nurturing influence of the railroad, the Montana and Minnesota Land and Improvement Company, and the personal interest of Frederick Billings himself.

Meanwhile, the Northern Pacific Railroad and the federal government engaged in vigorous boosterism, extolling the natural abundance of the entire region. Such propaganda mixed with romantic novels and overblown newspaper accounts to fuel the dreams of people seeking a better life. Hundreds of those dream seekers poured into Billings. By 1900, the population was over 3,000. During the next ten years, the town nearly burst its britches, growing 211 percent to have 10,000 residents by 1910. Promoters were calling Billings the Denver of the North.

Early Billings had all the familiar elements of a western boom town. Six-horse Concord stagecoaches boiled into town with passengers from Fort Benton and Great Falls. Prostitutes and gamblers strolled the streets, and vigilantes chased hobos out of town. Gunfights were a means of settling disputes. Cowboys trailed big herds of cattle into the railroad shipping yards, and Indians rode in from the plains to trade at the general stores.

Across the nation, the public soaked up pictures and stories like these and came to believe them as the whole truth. The complexity of the real west was overshadowed by its romantic images. Many of those images continue to hold a place in our collective subconscious.

Everyone knows the West looks like a Charlie Russell painting with wide open spaces where cowboys and Indians tear around on trusty ponies. Like a dime-store novel, the West is a wild and woolly land of adventure, excitement, and nature-in-the-raw. Like an old western movie, the West is a land of opportunity where sharp wits, hard work and guts never fail to make dreams come true.

It ain't always so. The story of Billings illustrates the often surprising realities behind the romance of the American West. Billings is surrounded by wide open spaces populated by cowhands and Indians, but they share the prairie with sheepherders, sugar beet farmers, oil and coal field workers, and Hutterites.

Open rangeland and homestead acts did provide a land of opportunity, but even sharp wits, hard work and guts weren't enough to protect livestock and homesteaders from nature-in-the-raw. Early day Billings did have its wild and woolly moments with shootouts, prostitutes, and lynchings, but it also had opera houses, Roman Catholic nuns, electric streetcars, and a central heating system for downtown businesses.

Today, images of the old west are blending with visions of the new west. Montana is once again attracting people looking for a better life. And, just like a hundred years ago, Billings holds some surprises for the dream seekers who come calling.

# Frederick Billings: A Powerful Mentor

*T*he town of Billings was named for one of the most quietly influential figures in America during the late 1800s. One of Frederick Billings' first accomplishments was graduating from the University of Vermont despite his family's rather threadbare circumstances. Two years later, in 1848, news of gold at Sutter's Mill in California prompted Billings to set out for California on borrowed money. To get there, he had to travel by steamship to Panama, cross Panama by canoe and mule, and then catch another steamer to San Francisco Bay.

Once in California, Billings never grubbed for gold. Instead, he was the first attorney to stake out an office in San Francisco. One of his first clients was John Sutter. Frederick Billings soon took on partners, and his firm of Halleck, Peachy and Billings became the most influential legal group in San Francisco.

The partners turned real estate litigation and investment into a gold mine of their own. One venture in particular made them all wealthy. Halleck, Peachy and Billings built and operated the famed Montgomery Block, a fire-proof office complex that became the commercial and social center of San Francisco.

By the age of 30, Frederick Billings had become a millionaire. He was active in California politics and was instrumental in establishing the University of California. In addition to building wealth and clout in California, Billings also built a reputation for integrity, fairness and generosity. He began a lifelong habit of giving freely to religious enterprises, universities, libraries and park projects. Billings also began cultivating his interests in experimental farming and conservation projects.

By 1865, at the age of 42, Billings had already retired from the practice of law. He was under consideration for a cabinet position in Abraham Lincoln's administration when the President was assassinated. Billings decided to pursue another of his interests, transcontinental railroads. Frederick Billings' business acumen and expertise in land law were perfect antidotes to the scandals and financial problems plaguing the Northern Pacific in 1873. During his nine-year tenure as president of the Northern Pacific, Billings was responsible for saving the railroad from collapse and for regaining public and Congressional support. Billings stepped down as president of the Northern Pacific in 1881, but he continued to be closely involved with the railroad.

Frederick Billings' sophisticated hand is evident in the planning and execution of the Billings townsite. Leapfrogging over Coulson surely had more to do with control and profit than any other considerations. After all, Coulson was located on the banks of a ready water supply, the Yellowstone River.

*Parmly Billings.* PERMANENT COLLECTION, WESTERN HERITAGE CENTER, BILLINGS

In contrast, Billings was two miles from the river, and water had to be hauled in and sold for 25 to 50 cents a barrel.

The Montana and Minnesota Land Improvement Company's ambitious plans for the valley soon addressed the city's water problem. Early in the spring of 1883, MMLI engineers started construction of an irrigation ditch from Young's Point (near Park City) to Billings. When the ditch was completed in July, it not only brought water to the city, but also irrigated MMLI land for nearly 40 miles along the valley. Irrigation would convert the dry alkali flats into fertile farmland.

Frederick Billings rarely visited his namesake town, but his influence was felt in nearly every aspect of its development. Under his direction, MMLI land prices were fair and reasonable. Billings' interests in scientific farming spilled over to the development of irrigated farms and the importation of new crops. And true to form, Frederick Billings donated generously to public education and single-handedly financed building the Congregational Church.

Billings' oldest son, Parmly, was the only Billings to

live in the city. Parmly and his cousin Edward Bailey moved to Billings in 1885 to take charge of Parmly's father's interests. In addition to managing the MMLI Company, Parmly and Bailey opened the city's second bank, The Bailey and Billings Bank. Frederick's money and expertise backed the venture.

At age 22, Parmly was a happy-go-lucky fellow who seemed to lack his father's knack for business. Parmly jovially called himself the family "reprobate." Perhaps both father and son hoped the "Magic City" of Billings would be the stepping stone to success for Parmly that the "Instant City" of San Francisco had been for Frederick. But Parmly died of kidney failure in 1888, after just three years in Billings. Between Parmly's death and his own in 1890, Frederick sold all the family's interests in the land and development company and the bank.

Other family members would write the Billings family's final chapter in the town's history. In 1901, Parmly's brother, Frederick Billings, Jr., donated nearly $30,000 to the city to build a public library as a memorial to Parmly. In 1913, Frederick Billings, Jr. died. Among his bequests was an additional $10,000 to the Parmly Billings library. In 1923, Elizabeth Billings gave over $20,000 to build a new wing on the library in memory of her brother Frederick Jr.

All together, the Billings family donated around $68,000 to the construction and support of the library. In the 1960s the Parmly Billings Library moved to larger, more modern quarters, but the original building still welcomes visitors as the Western Heritage Center.

*A statue of Frederick Billings guards the front of the Western Heritage Center, formerly the Parmly Billings Library.*
BOB ZELLAR

*In a vignette of Billings' mixture of agriculture and commerce, freight wagons filled with baled wool pass the Yegen Brothers Store, downtown Billings. Date unknown.* PERMANENT COLLECTION, WESTERN HERITAGE CENTER, BILLINGS

# Sharp Wits, Hard Work and Guts

*E*stablishing Billings as a railhead, or shipping center, destined it to serve a vast region. Transportation and commerce would become the driving forces behind the Billings economy, but ultimately, the town's survival rested on the agricultural fortunes of dream seekers spread across hundreds of miles of open plains. Businesses in Billings could prosper only if the surrounding cattle ranchers, wool growers and farmers prospered. The hard truth they all had to learn was that agricultural fortunes frequently ride the bucking broncs of boom and bust.

## Cowboys

Cowboys had begun trailing cattle into Montana from Texas in the 1870s. As the buffalo disappeared and the threat of Indian attacks lessened, the appeal of open grassland increased. Cattle could be fattened on the free range, then driven to railheads and shipped to market. Puffed-up literature like James Brisbin's 1881 *The Beef Bonanza or How to Get Rich on the Plains* helped lure speculators. Thousands upon thousands of Texas longhorns spent the best days of their lives grazing in Montana under the watchful guard of young hirelings called cowboys.

The arrival of the Northern Pacific Railroad in 1882 meant the cattle would no longer have to walk themselves to market. Within weeks of the railroad reaching Billings, cattle began to be shipped out. The first 700 head were part of a group of 2,000 cattle trailed in from western Montana. It was boom time for the cattle barons, but a cold-blooded bronc was about to bust up the party.

The winter of 1886–87 still stands as the worst on record. A storm began on Christmas Eve and for the next 60 days snow piled up and up, while temperatures dropped lower and lower. Parts of the state registered 55 degrees below zero, with a wind chill of 94 below. Around Billings, stage coaches stopped running, freight wagons were stranded, and trains derailed.

Livestock, unprotected on the open range, died. Nearly 60 percent of the cattle in Montana were lost in one winter. Such staggering losses ruined many investors and marked the end of the big trail drives.

Smaller herds provided with food and some shelter during the winter replaced the immense, free-ranging herds. Caring for the cattle fell more and more to the ranch families who owned them. Over time, the itinerant cowboys of western fame lost their place on the range.

Today, cattle ranching continues to be an economic mainstay of the region. Yellowstone County, which surrounds Billings, counts 173 ranches stretched over more than a million acres of range land, and more than 100,000 head of cattle and calves. Another half million head of cattle can be found on ranches within the 14-county primary trade area of Billings.

## Sheepherders

Although they rarely win starring roles in movies about the old west, sheep were an important factor in the frontier economy of eastern Montana. Sheep ranching began in earnest in 1882 when the railroad's presence provided a practical way to transport wool to eastern buyers. Just a year later, Billings was reported to be one of the largest inland wool markets in the world. During the hard winter of 1886–87, sheep fared better than cattle, prompting ranchers around Billings to further boost the size of their sheep bands.

In 1890, Frank Zimmerman used dynamite to build a trail up the side of the rimrocks west of Billings so he could drive his 2,200 sheep to summer pasture. Other ranchers owned flocks numbering 80,000 sheep or more. In 1910, Billings' wealthiest wool grower, Charles M. Bair, shipped out an incredible 47 train cars of wool shorn from his own sheep.

The large bands of sheep were cared for night and day by solitary herders. The herders lived in frontier-style mobile homes called sheepwagons. Competition for the grazing space often pitted sheepherders against their counterparts, the cowboys.

Somehow, sheepherders never managed to generate the romantic press cowboys did, and their place in history remains less glorified. But the reality and significance of sheep on the range can't be denied. By diversifying the agricultural base, sheep and wool production significantly strengthened the local economy.

From the heyday of the big flocks, sheep numbers gradually declined on the ranches around Billings. Today, Yellowstone County is home to about 12,000 sheep. But even with smaller numbers, regional sheep and wool production adds hundreds of thousands of dollars to the Billings-area economy every year.

## Homesteaders

Lured by promises of natural abundance and "free" land, thousands of farm families rode the rails into Bill-

ings during the early 1900s. Almost ten thousand filed for homesteads in the Billings area from 1909 to 1914. Several years of ample rainfall and mild winters gave promoters plenty of fodder for propaganda. A poster displayed throughout eastern states showed a plow in Montana turning over a furrow of gold coins.

In addition to homesteading, farmers were encouraged to purchase acreage from the Northern Pacific and its friends, like the Minnesota and Montana Land and Improvement Company. MMLI got into the act by issuing pamphlets with advice to "homeseekers and inves-

tors." The virtues of land near Billings were extolled and exaggerated.

Perhaps the biggest stretch was in describing the effects farming would have on annual rainfall. MMLI's pamphlet promised:

"While it has been demonstrated that the rainfall at present is sufficient to raise wheat and other crops, from 10 to 18 inches, it is bound to increase as the country is broken up…when the land is plowed and has a chance, there is bound to be a repetition of what occurred in South Dakota where the land now has to be [drain]tiled on account of the excessive rainfall."

*A timeless silhouette against the sunset.* JAMES WOODCOCK

*A worker stacks the product at Billings' sugar plant.* LARRY MAYER

At the turn of the century the majority of the American work force was still employed in agriculture, and the dream of owning land was pervasive. A small farm meant stability and independence. At least that's what people thought it meant. On the semiarid plains of the west, owning a small farm would mean backbreak, heartbreak and financial ruin for many. Once again it was nature-in-the-raw that busted the boom.

Homesteading reached a frenzied pitch in 1917 and 1918. The next three years brought gut-wrenching drought and insect plagues. What little produce homesteaders had to sell brought low prices on a depressed national market. In just four years, from 1921 to 1925, fifty percent of Montana's farmers lost their land to bankruptcy.

The drought years were to local farmers what the winter of 1886–87 had been to stock growers. Those who survived had to recognize the realities of Montana weather and adapt to it. Farmers adopted innovative dry-land (nonirrigated) farming techniques and increased their acreage, often by buying land from neighbors forced to leave. Today, many farm and ranch families trace their roots back to homesteaders who managed to hang on through the early 1900s.

Modern Yellowstone County has about 220,000 acres of dry-land fields under cultivation. Throughout the county and the broader trade area millions of bushels of winter wheat, barley, and oats are raised each year in dry-land fields.

## Sugar Beet Farmers

Could a real cowboy find happiness and success as a sugar beet farmer? It doesn't sound like a promising story line for a best-selling western novel, but it is exactly what happened in Billings. The real life cowboy was I.D. O'Donnell.

O'Donnell came to Montana in the early 1880s, hoping to make his fortune in the gold fields. Somewhere along the way, he took a job wrangling horses on the I.J. ranch north of Livingston. There, he became friends

63

with two other young men, Parmly Billings and his cousin, Edward Bailey.

Parmly and Bailey left the I.J. ranch when Frederick Billings put them in charge of the Montana and Minnesota Land and Improvement Company in the three-year-old town of Billings. About the same time, O'Donnell also decided to try his luck in the Magic City.

Through his association with Parmly and Bailey, O'Donnell gained a foothold in the business community of Billings. One of his first jobs was supervising construction of irrigation ditches MMLI was building throughout the valley. O'Donnell's involvement with irrigation led to other farming interests, including his experimental farm located just west of Billings near Hesper.

Within a few years, Parmly Billings was dead and Edward Bailey had moved on, but I.D. O'Donnell stayed to become the region's premier farmer and one of the city's most influential businessmen. In 1905, O'Donnell, P.B Moss, H.W. Rowley and others were instrumental in building a million dollar sugar factory on the south side of Billings.

Sugar beets and sugar refining were boons to the local economy. To sugar beet growers, blizzards were irrelevant; irrigation buffered against drought, and contracts with the sugar company buffered against market variables. It seemed sugar beet production would finally break the outlaw broncs of boom and bust.

Sugar beet farming is labor-intensive and seasonal workers were needed to thin, weed, and harvest the beets. The first workers were Japanese, followed the next season by German-Russian immigrants. Many German-Russian families who worked in the beet fields ultimately bought sugar beet farms of their own.

During World War I, another ethnic group came to the valley to work in the sugar beet fields. Farmers had greatly increased production to meet the wartime demand for agricultural products. The local work force wasn't sufficient to manage the harvest, so the Great Western Sugar Company, which bought the factory in 1918, brought in Mexican field hands. To house the workers and their families, Great Western provided raw materials and land for the Mexicans to build an adobe village southeast of the factory.

World War II brought together the most diverse group of field hands ever seen in the region. The majority of able-bodied men were away in military service, so many local women worked the fields along with an increased number of Mexican migrants. They were joined by Japanese-American volunteers released on work permits from the Heart Mountain relocation camp in northern Wyoming.

Italian and German prisoners of war (POWs) also worked in the beet fields. They had been assigned by the federal government to help ensure a successful harvest. Temporary POW camps were established to house the prisoners. Two were located in Billings—Italians on the campus of Rocky Mountain College, and Germans west of the sugar factory.

After the war, Mexican and Mexican-American workers dominated the migrant work force. Some found year-round work and chose to stay in the valley, forming a permanent Hispanic community in Billings. During the 1950s, Mexican families converted a local roller skating rink into Nuestra Señora de Guadalupe Catholic Church. The church served as the heart of Hispanic life in Billings for many years. It continues to sponsor an annual Mexican fiesta in South Park.

Resident Hispanics represent about one percent of the population of modern Billings. But Mexican-American migrants still make up more than 90 percent of the seasonal sugar beet workers in the Yellowstone Valley. From April through September, nearly 10,000 migrant workers live in the valley. Like other agricultural pursuits, sugar beet farming has developed into a sophisticated agribusiness. Inside the de-

*That lucrative crop: the sugar beet.*
LARRY MAYER

*Pastoral moonrise.* LARRY MAYER

*Why this fire company was parading in Billings in the late 1880s is unrecorded, but they were reviewed by a festive crowd.* MONTANA HISTORICAL SOCIETY

ceptively old-looking sugar factory is a state-of-the-art processing facility. Since 1986, the factory has been owned by Western Sugar, which is a subsidiary of Tate and Lyle, a multinational corporation and the world's largest manufacturer of sweeteners.

Company agriculturists oversee every aspect of growth and production in growers' fields. They perform soil analysis and specify everything from seed selection to use of herbicides and insecticides. Western Sugar contributes $45 million to $50 million each year in

grower contracts, payroll, and other payments to the Billings-area economy.

Even with its pivotal role in the local economy, most Billings residents' knowledge of the sugar industry boils down to the pungent aroma that pervades the south side of town while the factory is processing. It smells like an eccentric grandmother has come to town and is cooking up the world's biggest pot of beets.

## Immigrant Faces

Our images of the people who settled the West are often of English-speaking

white people of vague European descent. Reality is much more interesting than that.

The majority of people who settled in Billings were indeed white, but there was nothing vague about their backgrounds. They belonged to distinct ethnic groups: German, German-Russians, Scandinavians, Norwegians, Dutch, Irish, and English. They were often first or second generation immigrants who spoke their native languages, built their own churches, and nurtured their own prejudices against one another. The streets of early

Billings probably sounded more like the Tower of Babel than the soundtrack of television's "Gunsmoke."

While the adults worked to build their new lives, their children played with one another, went to school with one another, and eventually married one another. Gradually the original differences didn't seem so important.

In the Billings area today, whites make up 95 percent of the population and most are now of mixed European descent. But their rich cultural heritage is not forgotten. Many of the original ethnic names remain; the Sons of Norway organize each year to serve "Vikings on a stick" at MontanaFair; and nearby Red Lodge holds an annual Festival of Nations to celebrate the wonderful diversity of the original settlers.

Of course, not every newcomer to the Billings area was a white European. As early as 1898, the African Methodist Church was ministering to the spiritual needs of Billings' small black population. Chinese nationals came in with the railroad and some stayed to establish businesses, restaurants and other enterprises. In modern Billings, blacks and Asians account for about one percent of the population.

One group of immigrants that has stayed determinedly out of the melting pot is the Hutterites. Hutterites are German-speaking Anabaptists who live in communal farm colonies. The first Hutterite colonies in Montana were established during the 1940s. Hutterites embrace modern farm technology and the use of automobiles, but daily life is strictly regulated by centuries old religious tradition.

Members of the Golden Valley and Flat Willow colonies frequently come to Billings to purchase supplies and receive medical care. During the summer and fall, they also sell garden produce and homemade foods at the Farmer's Market in downtown Billings. Colony members are easy to distinguish. Men are usually bearded and wear black pants, jackets and hats. Hutterite women wear ankle-length skirts and colorful head scarves.

Like the Hutterites, contemporary farmers and ranchers throughout the region employ modern technology. Like the sugar company, they also utilize sophisticated agribusiness skills to survive in a global market. As much as ever, success on the prairie requires sharp wits, hard work and guts.

Psychologically as well as economically, Billings is still strongly tied to agriculture. Many Billings residents come from rural families. They have a close connection to the land and firsthand knowledge of what it takes to make a living out there.

# Indians

As thousands of dream-seeking immigrants stampeded onto the western frontier, the Plains Indians saw their dreams trampled into the dust. Confined to reservations, Indians faced not only the end of their dreams for the future, but also the destruction of their traditional way of life.

Like the people invading their lands, American Indians were not homogenous.

They, too, came from different tribal nations with different languages, religious beliefs, and traditions. They held prejudices and sometimes hatred against one another. Two nations, the Crow and Northern Cheyenne were assigned to reservations near Billings.

The Crow often came to Billings to trade and were frequently mentioned in newspaper accounts during

*Two Bears Lake, Beartooth Mountains.* JOHN REDDY

the 1880s and 1890s. The news articles reveal a checkered pattern of friendship and friction between the Crow people and area settlers.

The Crow were particularly loyal customers at Yegen's general store where the Crow language was spoken to make trading easier. The Crow also took part in fairs and celebrations in Billings. They were respected competitors in foot races, horse races, and wrestling matches. In 1892, when I.D. O'Donnell organized the first Yellowstone County Fair, the Crow people played a prominent role. Headed by Chief Plenty Coups, a Crow delegation camped at the fair grounds and took part in daily parades and events.

Other interactions were less congenial. In 1886, a U.S. Deputy Marshal named Quivey ordered local stock growers to stop grazing their herds on reservation land. The Crow were incensed because many of their people depended on the beef which stock growers provided in exchange for grazing privileges. A Crow leader, Chief Bobtail, came to Billings threatening to scalp Quivey.

A far more serious conflict occurred in 1887. Billings residents panicked at a rumor that the Crow warrior, Sword Bearer, and 200 followers were planning to raid the town. The raid never happened, but the incident inflamed anti-Indian sentiment among settlers. Even so, in 1893 a Billings sheriff arrested six white men accused of theft on the Crow reservation. The men were found guilty in U.S. district court and sentenced to prison.

Newsmaking clashes aside, it was less well-defined tensions that widened the rift between Indians and settlers. As the local economy changed from trapping and hunting to agriculture, the Indians' traditional skills became less and less valuable.

Gradually, the stagnant realities of reservation existence let a white man's plague more devastating than small pox seep into Indian life. Alcoholism and its ugly legacy would be passed from generation to generation. New stereotypes began to define the place of the warrior nations of the frontier. Within the space of a lifetime, the Plains Indians went from dominating the region to living on the fringes.

Today, American Indians make up about three percent of the population of Billings. Most are Crow or Northern Cheyenne, but there are also Sioux, Chippewa, Chippewa Cree, Mandan, Winnebago, Assiniboine, and others. As a group, Indians continue to face serious problems including: unemployment, poverty and educational deficits on the reservations; a high incidence of alcoholism; and prejudice.

As individuals, Indians in the Billings area live and work throughout the community. They include artists, fire fighters, administrators, politicians, and a Rhodes scholar. Annual events like the Crow Fair near Hardin and The Big Sky Indian Market in Billings draw large multi-ethnic crowds and help broaden understanding of both traditional and modern Indian life.

*1947 aerial of Billings looking north toward the airport. Photographer: K. F. Roahen, pilot: Tom Lynch.* COURTESY OF MRS. HERTHA LYNCH, BILLINGS

# Trading Post to Trade Center

*F*rom 1882 into the 1920s, Billings was a young town bursting with young people and new ideas. Residents were convinced nothing could stop their energetic little town from growing up to be the biggest and best city from here to Denver, or Spokane, or Minneapolis, or even Calgary.

With its false-fronted buildings along Montana and Minnesota Avenues, early Billings probably looked a lot like a typical movie set for the Old West. But inside the buildings and on the outskirts of town, the real-life supporting cast was writing its own script. Billings would change from a frontier trading post to an urban center for trade and manufacturing, and it wouldn't take long.

Billings' sphere of influence expanded with new railroad lines and improved roads. More and more, the hardworking people on the prairie looked to Billings for goods and services. Grocery staples, farm equipment, clothing, medical care, and even beer and cigars radiated out from Billings.

Wholesale as well as retail trade grew. Jobbing houses (small wholesalers) were established in Billings to serve the outlying areas. In 1910, Billings was home to more than 200 salesmen who traveled throughout eastern Montana and northern Wyoming peddling everything from shoes to farm implements.

In Billings, visitors and residents enjoyed the latest gadgets from the East. In 1887, Billings was among the first cities in the nation to have electric service, just five years behind New York and London. Telephones were introduced to Billings homes in 1890, and in 1907 the latest innovation, automatic dialing, was available. That same year, downtown businesses were equipped with central steam heat, delivered through pipes in underground tunnels.

By 1912, horses and buggies shared the streets of Billings with bicycles, automobiles, and six electric street cars. The battery-powered streetcars ran on tracks in the streets of central Billings. Fare was five cents. All these amenities plus elegant hotels like the Northern, ornate mansions, traveling the-

atrical productions, and an ever-growing variety of shops and stores built Billings' reputation as the cosmopolitan center of the region.

During the 1960s, Billings surpassed Great Falls to become Montana's largest town. Today, Billings is indeed the largest city between Denver, Calgary, Minneapolis and Spokane. People from 34 counties in Montana and Wyoming regularly come to Billings for business and pleasure. Retail sales exceed one billion dollars a year. A plethora of stores concentrate around 13 shopping areas, including the lively downtown area and two enclosed malls.

Manufacturing grew up right along with the city. A sandstone quarry and a brick plant provided customers with fireproof building materials (an important consideration in the flame-prone streets of early Billings). A flour mill and a creamery flourished near the sugar factory. In 1909, three railroad companies—the Northern Pacific, the Great Northern, and the Burlington—vied for the region's business.

By 1910, the city had six cigar factories and a collection of beer breweries. One brewery's sign was even more popular than its beer. People came from miles around to see the 920 electric lights on top of the Billings Brewery depict a beer bottle tipping to fill a glass. The breweries and cigar factories closed during Prohibition, but other enterprises were quick to take their places.

Today, Billings has over 200 manufacturing companies directly employing over 3,000 people. Goods ranging from sugar and hot cereal to jet fuel and sophisticated computer software are exported out of the city every day.

Billings is also the information center of the region. Three television stations, twelve radio stations and seven newspapers are headquartered in Billings. The *Billings Gazette* prints four regional editions and has a daily circulation of 60,000 newspapers in Montana, Wyoming and the Dakotas.

**Top left**: *Best friends enjoying a romp in Pioneer Park.* RICK GRAETZ
**Above:** *Madrigal Dinner performers at Eastern Montana College.*
MIKE SPRAGUE
**Left:** *The Castle, a historic home.*
JAMES WOODCOCK

**Facing page:** *In the Western Heritage Center.* LARRY MAYER

## The Underground Economy

In the 1920s, oil and natural gas added fuel to Billings' economic engine. Commercial oil production began in the Elk Basin on the Montana/Wyoming border in 1915. But it was the 1922 discovery of natural gas in Elk Basin that triggered an energy bonanza for eastern Montana. Developers built a two million dollar pipeline from the gas field to Billings, and by 1927 the city had 3,500 natural gas customers.

Petroleum soon outstripped natural gas in importance. In 1929, Yale Oil built the first of many small oil refineries in Billings. The conversion of crude oil to usable products added a major component to the Billings manufacturing community. At the same time, the prairie economy got a boost from jobs in exploration and drilling. Unfortunately, energy production, like agricultural production, would have to ride those same ornery broncs, boom and bust.

Billings galloped through the World War II years on the back of a boom in both agriculture and oil. The war effort guzzled incredible amounts of petroleum products and enabled Billings to solidify its position as the region's oil refining center. In 1954, a $20 million pipeline was built between Billings and Spokane, setting off another wild ride that lasted into the 1960s. Over the years, the area's small refineries were consolidated into three major operations, the Conoco and Exxon refineries in Billings, and the Cenex refinery in Laurel.

In the 1970s, Middle Eastern oil embargoes created a big demand for Montana oil and gas. Billings was riding high until oil prices took a nose dive in the mid-1980s. It was a fast, hard fall that knocked the wind out of the local economy. Almost overnight, Billings went from prosperity to recession. Hundreds of jobless residents packed their bags and filed out of town. Like all busts, this one left the Magic City battered and bruised, but smarter.

Despite the bust, none of the refineries went out of business, and a river of oil continued flowing through the pipeline. In the 1990s, more than five million barrels of crude oil a day pour into the three Billings-area refineries. Converted to gasoline, diesel and jet fuel, asphalt, propane, and other products, oil leaves Billings through a second system of underground pipelines. All together, petroleum activities pump hundreds of millions of dollars into the regional economy annually. The refineries alone are responsible for approximately $165 million a year in local payroll, taxes, and other payments.

Coal also has played an important role in the economic development of eastern Montana and Billings. In the 1880s, Frederick Billings invested in land in the Bull Mountains because of coal deposits there. Coal dug out of hillsides provided fuel for settlers on the treeless plains. But coal mining didn't significantly impact the regional economy until the 1970s, when the national energy crisis made large scale strip mining economically feasible.

By 1979, 32.5 million tons of coal were being produced in eastern Montana mines. Most of it was exported for use by out-of-state power companies, but some large power plants were built in Montana. Today, the Montana Power Company operates a coal- and gas-powered electric generation plant in Billings, and four units in Colstrip, Montana. Montana Power Company provides electricity to Billings residents and thousands of others living in its 107,600-square-mile service area.

The 1990 Federal Clean Air Act once again pushed Montana's and Wyoming's low-sulfur coal into the national spotlight. Low-sulfur coal produces less pollution when burned than does the high-sulfur coal produced in eastern mines.

Even so, natural gas may be the rising star of Montana's fossil fuels. Its clean burning and relatively low cost make it environment- and consumer-friendly. The Williston Basin on the Mon-

*Chapple Brothers Drug Company, created by two doctors, may have been the beginning of Billings becoming a center for medical services.* COURTESY PARMLY BILLINGS LIBRARY

tana/North Dakota border currently provides natural gas to a wide region, including Billings, through a system of 4,100 miles of underground pipes.

## Medical Services

Billings' evolution as a regional center for trade and manufacturing paralleled its evolution as a regional health care center. In 1893, the Chapple brothers opened a drugstore on Montana Avenue. Two of the brothers, Henry and James were doctors. They used the store as a

sort of frontier emergency room, where the injured were taken for treatment. The drugstore successfully operated for over 60 years, but within a few years the townspeople wanted a real hospital.

In 1896, Dr. Henry Chapple was not only the town surgeon, but also the mayor. He undertook a thousand-mile trip to Leavenworth, Kansas to beseech the Sisters of Charity of Leavenworth to open a hospital in Billings. Already active in schools and hospitals in the

western part of the state, the sisters agreed. When Sister Mary Anacleta and Sister Mary Lawrence arrived in Billings, they found patients waiting for them in a downtown building.

With the help of the entire community, the first Saint Vincent Hospital was constructed and opened by February of 1899. Seven more sisters arrived to help staff the 40-bed hospital. The nuns did most of the heavy physical work of the hospital, including clearing away brush and debris so they

**Top left:** *In 1991, the traveling Montana Cup Golf Tournament—for the state's top 10 pro and top 10 amateur male golfers—came to Billings' semi-private Briarwood Country Club.* JAMES WOODCOCK
**Top right:** *Yellowstone National Park's northeast entrance is only three hours drive for Billings recreationists.* JOHN REDDY
**Bottom:** *Deaconess Medical Center atrium. The original Deaconess hospital was founded in 1927.* JAMES WOODCOCK

**Left:** *Chamber of Commerce Building.* JOHN REDDY

**Below:** *Commercial flight approaching Logan International Airport atop the rims.* MICHAEL CRUMMETT

could raise garden vegetables and poultry for themselves and their patients.

These women would have been perfect subjects for a Charlie Russell sketch. Had he known, he might have swapped them a drawing for one of the precautionary tickets they offered in the fall of 1899. According to the hospital's ad in the *Billings Gazette*, "Single men and women can, by the payment of $10, obtain a ticket which will entitle them to free care and nursing for a year."

The Sisters of Charity weren't the only women doing medical work in Billings. In 1898, a husband and wife team, physicians Andrew and Harriet Clark, opened offices in Billings. Harriet practiced gynecology, obstetrics and pediatrics, and Andrew specialized in surgery. The Clarks practiced in Billings for over 40 years.

Another Billings physician, Dr. Louis Allard, came to Billings in 1916. Allard helped Billings face one of its worst medical crises, a polio epidemic. Hundreds of area children were crippled. In 1923, Saint Vincent Hospital moved into a new, larger building, and under Allard's direction the old hospital was converted into a hospital-school for disabled children. The children lived at the school, receiving medical treatment while keeping up with their education. A flood in 1939 forced the school to close.

In 1917, Drs. A.J. Movius and J.H. Bridenbaugh opened a joint practice in Billings that eventually grew into the region's largest multi-specialty group practice, the Billings Clinic. Deaconess Hospital opened in 1927, providing Billings with an additional 58 hospital beds.

Today, Saint Vincent Hospital and Health Center and Deaconess Medical Center are state-of-the art regional medical centers. Together they provide nearly 600 hospital beds in the heart of Billings' 35-block medical corridor.

Along with the hospitals, more than 20 health-related facilities are located in the corridor, including the Northern Rockies Cancer Center, and several mental health and psychiatric centers.

Billings' excellent medical facilities and hundreds of physicians (representing 46 specialties) draw patients from within a 250-mile radius. In a time when small rural hospitals are closing their

doors, Billings is a medical mecca for rural families from throughout the region.

## Travel and Tourism

Travel and tourism further strengthen and diversify the Billings economy. Montana's natural beauty enchanted early visitors, but it took the railroads to open the way for sightseers. Frederick Billings recognized the value of an alliance between tourism, commerce and conservation. While planning the railroad's route, he considered conservation of the region's beauty as well as the needs of businesses and tourists.

Frederick Billings was behind the first Northern Pacific guide books and photographs that helped draw tourists through the area on their way to Yellowstone National Park. He also hoped to have historical markers placed along the railroad's route, including one at Pompeys Pillar, just east of Billings. The Northern Pacific never followed through on Frederick Billings' entire plan, but a protective screen

was placed over Captain William Clark's signature on Pompeys Pillar. The signature is still visible today, thanks in part to the efforts of Frederick Billings and the Northern Pacific.

The rapidly growing popularity of automobile travel led to better highways and Billings was at the intersection of five of them in 1920s. In 1923, the city put out a welcome mat to travelers in the form of the "Tourist Park" campground (now North Park). That first year, about 12,000 visitors took advantage of the city's hospitality.

Nineteen sixty-two was a banner year for tourism in Billings. Seattle was hosting the World's Fair, and thousands of families drove through Billings on their way to the Fair. Many paid $1.75 to spend the night at a Billings campground equipped with hot showers, clean bathrooms and a little store. Travelers were so delighted with the simple amenities that a new business was born. Based on that summer's success, Billings businessman Dave Drum launched a system of highway campgrounds called Kampgrounds of America or KOA.

The Billings hotel and motel industry traces its roots back to the town's earliest days with hotels built for railroad passengers and workers. Some establishments provided basic lodging, but others like the Grand and Northern Hotels were spacious and lavishly decorated. The original Northern Hotel was built in 1904. It had more than 70 guest rooms, a grand lobby, and a penthouse apartment. A spectacular fire in 1940 destroyed the original Northern Hotel, but it was immediately rebuilt and is still considered one of Billings' finest hotels.

Of course, the Northern has plenty of competition. Modern Billings has nearly 3,500 motel and hotel rooms available for tourists and convention-goers.

## Air Travel

Today, many Billings visitors arrive by plane, landing atop the Rims at Billings Logan International Airport. The airport is a regional hub for air traffic. Commuter lines feed passengers from throughout the region into Billings, where they can make connections to major metropolitan areas. Nonstop service between Billings and Denver, Salt Lake City or Minneapolis takes less than two hours. Seven airlines, including four major carriers, operate approximately 30 passenger flights in and out of Billings each day.

In the early 1990s, a $20 million renovation and expansion project enhanced the terminal's efficiency and aesthetics. The airport's accessibility is a pleasant bonus for business passengers and tourists alike. It's only fifteen minutes from most parts of Billings and just five minutes from downtown offices. More than a quarter of a million passengers use the airport each year. Most take for granted the marvels of flight.

It was different in 1912 when excited crowds gathered to watch Billings' first pilot, dentist Frank Bell, fly his open Curtiss Biplane. Bell made round trips to Laurel and Park City at the breathtaking speed of 60 miles per hour. Ten years later, Billings residents thrilled to wing-walking stunts and parachute jumps performed by another pilot, Charles Lindbergh. Lindbergh, one of the most romantic figures in aviation history, worked in Billings for three months as a garage mechanic before floating away down the Yellowstone River in a leaky boat.

# Youthful Vigor

Many of the people who transformed Billings from a trading post to a trade center were in only their twenties or early thirties when they began making things happen in the Magic City. Parmly Billings was 22. A.L. Babcock, later known as "Mr. Billings," was 31. But three young men, Henry Ward Rowley, Ignatius D. O'Donnell and Preston Boyd Moss were particularly powerful.

Rowley, O'Donnell and Moss were involved in nearly every major enterprise in Billings including real estate development, banking, farming and ranching, the sugar factory, and the city's water, power and telephone companies. All three men were also generous supporters of Billings churches, hospitals and the Polytechnic College (now Rocky Mountain College).

H.R. Rowley was 22 years old when he first came to the Billings area as an engineer for the Northern Pacific Rail-

*Henry Ward Rowley.* COURTESY PARMLY BILLINGS LIBRARY

road in 1880. After the town was established in 1882, Rowley took a job with the Minnesota and Montana Land and Improvement Company (MMLI). He and O'Donnell formed the Suburban Homes Company that bought out MMLI holdings in 1890. Rowley's activities also included involvement in the Merchants National Bank, the Commercial Club, and the Billings Street Car Company. H.R. Rowley died in Billings in 1931 at the age of 74.

I.D. O'Donnell came to Billings in 1884 at the age of 25. He became an agricultural and civic leader. In 1907, O'Donnell was instrumental in establishing the nation's first federal reclamation project, the irrigated farms of the Huntley Project. He also brought the 1909 Dry Land Farming Congress to Billings. The Department of Interior appointed O'Donnell supervisor of irrigation for 17 western states in 1916. *Country Gentleman Magazine* named him "Best Farmer in Montana" in 1919.

I. D. O'DONNELL

*Ignatius D. O'Donnell.* COURTESY
PARMLY BILLINGS LIBRARY

O'Donnell organized the first
Yellowstone County Fair,
and later founded the Mid-
land Empire Fair which grew
into today's MontanaFair.
I.D. O'Donnell died in Billings at the age of 87 in 1948.

P.B. Moss was 29 when he
rode the train into Billings in
1892. Just a year later, he
was vice-president of the
First National Bank, and
was president by 1896. In
the early 1900s, Moss and
a partner, T.A. Snidow,
owned 80,000 head of
sheep. From 1908 to 1914,
Moss owned the *Billings
Gazette*. He and Rowley
built the first Northern
Hotel in 1904, and an elderly
P.B. Moss rebuilt the hotel
after the original was destroyed by fire in 1940. Like
his associates, Moss built a
grand mansion west of downtown Billings. P.B. Moss died
in Billings in 1947 at the age
83.

*Preston Boyd
Moss.*
COURTESY MOSS
MANSION

# Saloons, Opera Houses and a Normal School

*The horseback rider is coming north on Broadway in this picture taken sometime between 1906 and 1918.*
COURTESY SENIA C. HART AND THE WESTERN HERITAGE CENTER, BILLINGS

*T*he hurly-burly air of Billings' early days was thick with gamblers, tramps, prostitutes and drunks. The citizenry often sought relief from the dusty streets in the city's many saloons. Poker games, horse racing, fighting and bordello diversions were staple forms of entertainment in young Billings. This gloriously debauched vision of the wild west is jarred a little by the fact that the new town also supported an opera house. The Boston Comic Opera presented a musical show there shortly after the railroad reached Billings in 1882. A second theater, the Variety, opened a few months later and advertised "A Galaxy of Stars." Unfortunately, these theaters were in a rough part of town and respectable women never patronized them.

Surprisingly enough, there were at least as many respectable women (and men) in Billings as otherwise. They built churches, organized schools, and had their own sort of fun. The town's rowdiest elements were not particularly welcome at picnics, ice cream socials, tableaus, bazaars and dances sponsored by the Congregational, Episcopalian or Catholic congregations. The solid citizens of Billings worked hard to bring culture and sophistication to the rough-edged boom town, and they succeeded. Near the turn of the century, education, music, theater, and art thrived right along with traditional western events like fairs, rodeos and saloon hopping.

In entertainment, like so many other areas, early-day Billings undermines our stereotypes of the Old West. Bicycle racing was an official fair event in 1894, and in 1907 Billings had an under-ground bowling alley and shopping mall. Perhaps even more disconcerting to believers of the myth is the roller skating rink that was popular in Billings during the 1880s. Imagine a room full of range-hardened, bow-legged cowpokes whooping it up by learning how to roller skate. Cowboys in the saloons, sure. Cowboys at the church picnic, maybe. But, cowboys on wheels? Unbelievable!

## Theaters

In 1895, A.L. Babcock built Billings a beautiful (and thoroughly respectable) opera house. Residents routinely filled its 800 seats to see some of the finest touring acts in the nation. In 1906, Babcock's Opera House burned down. He rebuilt, calling the new structure the Babcock Theatre.

After years as a showcase for live theater in Billings, the Babcock was converted to a movie house. Then, in the early 1990s, the Babcock was closed. Billings residents organized to save the beautiful and historic old theater. They reopened the Babcock as a classic movie house and stage for live theater.

Another historic Billings movie theater was rescued from destruction by the community in the mid-1980s. The lavish Fox Movie Theater was built in 1931. Its art deco design thrilled Depression-weary residents, but movie palaces eventually fell out of vogue. The Fox faced a bleak future until a $5.2 million refurbishing project, completed in 1987, transformed the aging Fox into a showcase.

The faded movie house glittered into new life as the Alberta Bair Theater for the Performing Arts. Attracting national and regional touring groups, the theater presents the top professional productions in ballet, opera, dance, theater, and music, as well as community events. The Alberta Bair Theater is a regional focal point for the performing arts, hosting more than 100 events a year.

The theater's renovation is a sterling example of Billings' community spirit and commitment to the arts. Money for the theater was raised during the mid-1980s when Billings was in the midst of a recession in oil, gas and agriculture. Even in such gloomy times, Billings residents viewed their city with pride, and took an active role in making good things happen. From small contributions and the generosity of Alberta Bair herself, the community opened and supported Montana's finest performing arts center.

As busy as the Babcock and Alberta Bair Theaters are, they are not the only places to find live entertainment in Billings. The 12,000-seat MetraPark enclosed arena draws thousands of people each year to concerts, circuses, trade shows, ice shows, rodeos and other

*Right:* MontanaFair.
JAMES WOODCOCK
*Below:* *Little League softball.*
J. MARK KEGANS
*Bottom:* *Billings and its rimrocks after an afternoon shower.*
LARRY MAYER

84

events. The entire Metra-Park, including fairground buildings, grandstand and race track, accommodates nearly 650 events each year.

The Billings Studio Theater showcases local talent with a full season of plays presented in its own 250 seat theater. Children's theater groups, a jazz and blues society, dinner theaters, college performances, a community band, community orchestra, symphony orchestra, and a wide variety of other musical groups make almost any evening in Billings a smorgasbord of live entertainment.

The Billings Symphony is a favorite choice for music afi-cionados. The roots of the symphony go all the way back to Billings' earliest days when immigrants brought a variety of musical instruments to the city. By 1883, Billings residents had organized a brass band. The city's first orchestra was formed in 1889, but it was a males-only affair, in terms of both performers and audience members.

By 1909, the Billings College of Music was offering lessons, concerts and recitals to both sexes. In 1913, 42 musicians formed a concert band, and the Babcock Theatre had its own orchestra to accompany productions there. Billings' first symphony orchestra was organized in the 1920s.

The current Billings Symphony is an award-winning organization of more than 70 musicians. From its home at the Alberta Bair Theater, the Billings Symphony offers an array of performances including classical works, pops and original compositions. Each summer the symphony treats residents to a free concert under the trees of Pioneer Park.

## A Normal School and a Polytechnic Institute

The arts in Billings are greatly enriched by the presence of two colleges. Stu-

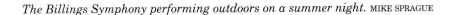

*The Billings Symphony performing outdoors on a summer night.* MIKE SPRAGUE

dents from both Rocky Mountain College and Eastern Montana College offer stage and musical productions. Faculty members are involved in arts projects throughout the city. The colleges sponsor camps, workshops, and cultural events for area schools and members of the general public.

## Rocky Mountain College

Rocky Mountain College got its start as the Billings Polytechnic Institute in 1908. Brothers Ernest and Lewis Easton founded the private Christian college. Originally, courses focused on practical sciences, particularly agriculture. The school operated a ranch and dairy farm for educational purposes.

Students also raised and canned great quantities of garden vegetables and fruit. The college's flour and cereal mill was later converted to one of Billings' most popular restaurants, aptly named The Granary.

Today, Rocky Mountain College is a four-year, fully accredited liberal arts college. It retains its Christian heritage with affiliations to the United Church of Christ, the United Methodist Church and the Presbyterian Church. With a total enrollment of over 800 students, the college attracts students from throughout Montana as well as over 40 other states and several foreign countries.

Most buildings on the 60-acre campus are made of na-

tive sandstone. In its early days, the school operated its own sandstone quarry and many campus structures were built by students. The campus' tree-lined front commons is the site of Summer-Fair, an annual outdoor arts and crafts show popular with Billings residents.

## Eastern Montana College

Eastern Montana College (EMC) had its beginnings in 1927 as a Normal School, or teachers college. The first faculty members held classes for 135 students in rented rooms. It wasn't until 1931 that the college had its own buildings. In the mid-1930s, construction of campus facilities was expedited by projects directed by both the Civil Works Administration and the Public Works Administration. By 1937, 400 students were attending classes on campus.

Enrollment at Eastern Montana College (EMC) is now around 4,000 students. It is a fully accredited, multi-purpose college—the third largest in the Montana University System. EMC offers associate and bachelor degrees in arts and sciences, business, education and human services. Montana State University operates a satellite nursing program at EMC. Masters degrees can be earned in education and human services. Through cooperation with the University of Montana and the Uni-

versity of Arizona, Eastern Montana College is also able to offer graduate degrees in business administration and library science.

Among EMC's many cultural contributions to the community is the operation of public radio station KEMC. Affiliated with National Public Radio and American Public Radio, KEMC broadcasts classical music, jazz, news and public affairs programs. Twenty-one translators throughout Montana and northern Wyoming extend KEMC's range to encompass the largest geographical area of any public radio station in the United States.

Each summer, the EMC campus hosts the annual Big Sky Indian Market sponsored by the Native American Cultural Institute of Montana. The market revolves around an art show featuring the works of contemporary artists of Northern Plains heritage. Activities, demonstrations, dances, and speakers provide further opportunities for firsthand experiences with both traditional and modern Indian culture.

In addition to Eastern Montana and Rocky Mountain colleges, Billings has a small Baptist college and several trade and industrial schools. The Billings Vocational Technical Center offers several post-secondary degree and certificate programs. Other trade schools in Billings prepare students for careers in hair styling, modeling, business, and aviation. Billings is also home to the Western College of Auctioneering.

## A Tradition of Educational Excellence

Billings' elementary and secondary schools, both public and private, have always been a source of community pride. Composite test scores for elementary students are in the top twenty percent of the nation. Composite ACT scores in Billings' high schools are also above the national average.

Private schools in Billings include a Montessori school, two Lutheran schools, a Seventh Day Adventist school and the Billings Christian School. The Billings Unified Catholic Schools represent the largest private school system in the city. From preschool through 12th grade, the Catholic schools have a combined enrollment of nearly one thousand children.

## Museums

Children and adults alike enjoy Billings' museums. The Peter Yegen/Yellowstone County Museum documents western life near the turn of the century. The heart of the museum is an 1893 log cabin that originally served as a community social center in downtown Billings. It was moved to its present location near the airport in 1953. Outside the cabin sits one of the last coal-fired steam engine locomotives used by the Northern Pacific, "Old 1031."

Another place to find exhibits of the area's rural heritage is Oscar's Dreamland. The privately owned Museum of Yesteryear has ten restored historical buildings including Yellowstone County's first schoolhouse. Nineteen acres of antique farm equipment, cars, covered wagons, and tools are also on display.

*This photograph of the Moss Mansion, dated 1910, is the only known one that includes the large sandstone barn west of the home.*
COURTESY MOSS MANSION

*The Moss Mansion Christmas lights.* LARRY MAYER

***Facing page, top left:*** *Rocky Mountain College, Eaton Hall.* BOB ZELLAR
***Top right:*** *Interior, Yellowstone Art Center.* JOHN REDDY
***Bottom:*** *Eastern Montana College.* BOB ZELLAR

The Western Heritage Center is located in the original Parmly Billings library built in 1901. The Center works to preserve and record regional history. A wide collection of historic photographs and memorabilia are safeguarded at the Western Heritage Center. Changing exhibits allow visitors to explore various facets of Montana's past and present.

P. B. Moss's mansion on Division Street was on the farthest reaches of Billings when it was built in 1902. Today, Division Street marks the western boundary of the central business district. Moss hired H.J. Hardenberg, designer of the original Waldorf-Astoria Hotel in New York City, to design the three-story residence.

Red sandstone from near Lake Superior was imported for the exterior walls. The elegant interior includes a Moorish entry hall, two parlors, a music room, conservatory, six bedrooms, and three bathrooms. Servants' quarters and a never-completed ballroom occupy the third floor. Opened to the public in 1987, the restored mansion lets visitors step back into Billings' history.

The old Yellowstone County Jail took on a decidedly different clientele when it was converted to the Yellowstone Art Center. The Center's permanent Montana collection features exceptional works from modern regional artists. The museum also displays traveling exhibits of contemporary or historical significance.

## ZooMontana

If you like your history on the hoof, there's no better place than Billings' exciting new wildlife park, ZooMontana. The $4.5 million zoo, which opened in 1993, is located just west of Billings on Shiloh Road. The 70-acre zoo site is a combination of open and wooded terrain incorporated into a variety of natural habitat exhibits and nature trails.

Canyon Creek meanders through the grounds and helps form many of the exhibit areas. Deer, beaver, waterfowl and other wildlife, naturally present on the zoo site before construction began, continue to find safe haven. Parts of the site are set aside as sanctuary for these free-roaming native species.

A sensory garden with special considerations for the visually impaired and wheelchair bound is the first exhibit visitors encounter inside the zoo. Further along is the Montana Homestead exhibit, complete with farm animals to touch and pet. From the homestead, visitors move on to see exhibits of both native and exotic species such as river otters, waterfowl and Siberian tigers. All animals living at the park are native to climates similar to that of the Billings area.

Implementation of the complete master plan for the zoo is scheduled to take place over several years. As exhibits are completed, visitors will get an intriguing and educational look at grizzly bears, wolves, bactrian camels, snow monkeys, antelope, deer, bison, elk, fish, reptiles and insects. ZooMontana raises funds for new exhibits, in part, by sponsoring two of Billings' favorite entertainment events, the outdoor ZooGrass Festival in June and the Boo-at-the-Zoo carnival for kids at Halloween.

## Fairs and Rodeos

No western town is complete without fairs and rodeos, and Billings' MontanaFair is the state's largest. Held in August at MetraPark, the fair highlights modern agriculture and attracts over 600 thousand people each year. In October, the region's largest stock show is held at MetraPark. The annual Northern International Livestock Exposition (NILE) includes five nights of rodeo action. Rodeo events can also be seen every summer night at the Billings Night Rodeo, located south of Interstate 90 at the King Avenue exit.

City residents and visitors enjoy a variety of other annual events including: Billings' Western Days in June, Huntley Projects' Homesteader Days in July, Red Lodge's Mountain Man Rendezvous in July and Festival of Nations in August, and Laurel's Herbstfest in Sep-

*The Yegen Brothers Implement Company was one of the victims of early-day Billings fires.* PERMANENT COLLECTION, WESTERN HERITAGE CENTER, BILLINGS

tember. The Crow Fair is held at Crow Agency each August. During the fair, Crow Agency becomes the largest American Indian encampment in the world. Participants and guests enjoy tribal dancing, singing, and an all-Indian rodeo.

## Restaurants and Casinos

Billings has over 150 restaurants. Many of the city's finest restaurants have special appeal because they are located in buildings dating back to the turn of the century. Adventuresome diners can take a culinary tour through ethnic restaurants featuring Italian, Irish, Dutch, Mexican, Chinese (Mandarin, Cantonese and Szechuan), Cajun, Thai, Greek or Japanese food.

Gambling machines (and limited live games) were legalized in Montana in the 1980s. Many restaurants and lounges now have a poker machine or two on-site. Casinos offers rows and rows of gambling machines, often luring patrons in with low-priced food and drinks. It seems gambling is just as popular today as it was back in the 1880s. And, as a matter of fact, saloons have remained remarkably popular too.

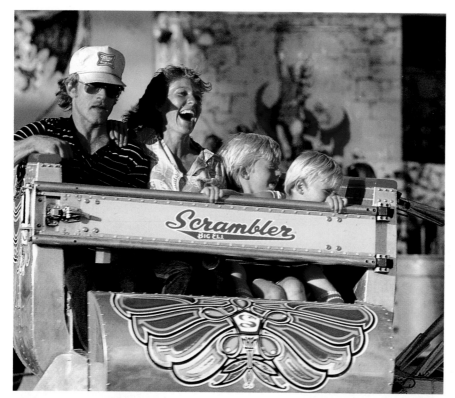

*Enjoying the MontanaFair.*
LARRY MAYER

**Above:** *A rodeo clown has a full-time job with Billings' generous summer rodeo schedule.*
BOB ZELLAR
**Left:** *The annual ZooGrass Festival in June raises money for Billings' wildlife park, ZooMontana.* BOB ZELLAR

# Romancing the West:
# Will James and J.K. Ralston

Many of our favorite images of the old west were created by artists and authors, like Charlie Russell, who actually lived and worked on the range. Billings was home to two men whose work also contributed to the those indelibly romantic impressions of the American West.

Will James became famous in the 1920s as a cowboy author and illustrator. His work reflects his passion for horses and cowboys. Of

James' 24 popular books, the most famous was *Smoky, the Cowhorse* published in 1926. *Smoky* received the prestigious Newberry Award for best book of children's literature from the American Library Association.

Interestingly, James' own life story illustrates how western romance can sometimes overpower reality. He was born in the eastern Canadian province of Quebec in 1892 as Ernest Nephtali Dufault. When he was 15 years old, he ran away from home to become a cowboy, spending his teens and twenties working on ranches in the American West.

As a cowboy, Dufault changed his name to Will James and went on to create a whole new identity for himself. In his 1930 autobiography, *Lone Cowboy*, James claims he was born in the back of a wagon in Montana and describes his childhood "amongst cowboys and trappers." For the rest of his life, James went to great lengths to prevent anyone from

*Will James.* PERMANENT COLLECTION, WESTERN HERITAGE CENTER, BILLINGS

learning the truth about his background.

In 1927, James purchased a ranch south of Billings. For the next 10 years, his popularity was at a peak and he feverishly produced books and magazine articles to finance his Rocking R Ranch. He also drank feverishly. Ultimately, alcoholism cost James the ranch and his wife. Alone, he moved to a house in Billings and continued to work.

At the age of 50, Will James died and, as he requested, his ashes were scattered over his Billings home and ranch. The city changed the name of the street he had lived on to Smoky Lane, and his former home, 3106 Smoky Lane is still occupied as a private residence.

J.K. (Ken) Ralston was a talented Montana cowboy who became a distinguished regional artist. Ralston lived and worked in Billings from 1937 until his death in 1987. He and Will James were casually acquainted, primarily through their mutual friend and patron Earl Snook. Ironically, Ralston's youth was nearly everything James wished his had been.

Ralston was born to a pioneering Montana family in 1896. His grandfather had come to the mining camps of Alder Gulch in 1864. Young Ken was raised amongst miners and cowboys. He grew up near Helena and Sidney and worked for many years as a cowboy.

Starting out on his artistic career, Ralston worked at commercial art throughout the Northwest, painting signs on bars, cafes, barn roofs, and storefronts. In the early 1930s, he painted gasoline pumps for Yale Oil of Billings. But as his reputation grew, Ralston focused on western art.

He was frequently commissioned to paint historical murals on banks and public buildings. His mural depicting Dr. Frank Bell making Billings' first airplane flight was painted in the 1940s for the Billings airport and is still on display there. Among the exhibits at the Little Bighorn Battlefield is a mural Ralston painted in 1965 portraying the final moments of the battle. He also illustrated several books, including his own *Rhymes of a Cowboy* in 1969.

Ultimately, Ralston's work earned him many awards, including his 1978 induction into the National Cowboy Hall of Fame of Great Westerners. That same year, he received the William F. Cody Award of Excellence in Art from the Old West Trail Association and in 1984, the Montana Arts Council awarded Ralston the Governor's Award for Distinguished Achievement in the Arts.

In 1987, at the age of 91, J.K. Ralston died in Billings. His studio cabin on Grand Avenue was moved to the campus of Rocky Mountain College. Plans are now underway to incorporate the studio into a center for the exhibition and promotion of regional western art.

*J.K. Ralson in his log-cabin studio, circa 1984.* JO RAINBOLT

# Law and Order

*Soldiers escorted engineer W.H. Norton to the Grand Hotel after he drove in the first train following the 1894 railroad strike. Calamity Jane is said to be the woman among these soldiers.* COURTESY PARMLY BILLINGS LIBRARY

*F*rontier boom towns are renowned for gunfights, shoot-outs, and vigilante justice. Billings was no exception. The city's phenomenal growth and access to good transportation made it as popular with criminals as it was with honest business people.

It was the rowdy town of Coulson, however, that first found need of a cemetery. By the spring of 1882, 21 victims of gunplay rested at Boot Hill on the bluffs above Coulson. Things were so bad that the townspeople petitioned for a deputy sheriff. Muggins Taylor was appointed. He was a former army scout who had carried the news of Custer's massacre in from the battlefield. Taylor took office in May, only to be shot and killed in September—and buried at Boot Hill.

After Taylor's death, a new deputy was quickly named. This one had a truly grisly reputation. John "Liver-Eating" Johnson was a mountain man whose pregnant wife had been killed by a Crow war party in 1847. In revenge, Johnson went on his own warpath. He killed Crow warriors whenever he could, then cut out their livers and rubbed the blood in his long beard. Johnson eventually gave up his vendetta against the Crow, but in the 1880s he further embellished his reputation by eating the heart and liver of a freshly butchered steer at a fair in Billings.

Liver-Eating Johnson's fearsome reputation didn't seem to pose much of a deterrent to the gun-happy populace, however. Shortly after Liver-Eating took office, James D. Russell was shot and killed in a Billings billiard parlor. Russell's death earned him the distinction of being Billings' first homicide victim. A month later, railroad section hands used gunfire to settle their Christmas morning differences. Despite the continuing deaths and street brawls, the optimistic editor of the *Billings Post* wrote that "Billings was essentially peaceable."

Things did begin to settle down a bit in 1883. There was a report in May of a reckless cowboy fined five dollars for riding through town shooting off his gun. In October, when the first district court convened in the city, there were nine criminal cases, ten civil suits, and six divorces, but no murder trials. Even so, the city felt obliged to spend $10,000 on a jail that opened for occupancy in January 1885.

Two ordinances passed in 1886 indicated that law-abiding residents were beginning to get the upper hand. The city council prohibited minors from visiting saloons and also prohibited shopkeepers from endangering pedestrians by hanging signs over the sidewalk.

## Vigilante Justice

In 1888, hobos and tramps hitching rides into Billings on the railroad were considered a menace to the community. Residents organized a vigilance committee to round up the drifters every morning and help them out of town. The dangers of both hobos and vigilance committees became clear on July 23, 1891. Two hobos killed saloon keeper Joseph Clancy by beating his head in with a beer mallet.

One of the murderers got away and the other was arrested. Clancy's death enraged the community, for he was a well-respected resident and the father of two children. That night, an angry mob stormed the jail and dragged out the accused man, known only as John Doe. The mob lynched the hobo from a telegraph pole near a railroad crossing and left the body swinging for all to see until the next afternoon. Billings Sheriff John Ramsey denounced the hanging and it remains the only time a Billings mob killed a jailed suspect.

Sheriff Ramsey remained in office and continued to lead a busy and dangerous life. He tracked down horse thieves, train robbers and more murderers. In 1894, Ramsey's peacekeeping skills faced new challenges. First, striking miners from Butte came through town in a stolen train. Later, a strike by the American Railway Union stopped train traffic along the entire route and sorely divided the citizens of Billings. Three hundred local union members joined the strike. There were threats to blow up railroad bridges and tunnels. In September, army troops from Fort Custer were stationed outside of Billings to guard the tracks and force strikers back to work.

Nineteen hundred eight brought another incident of vigilante justice. It began when Sheriff John T. Webb was murdered by a sheepherder resisting arrest. A posse of local men discovered Webb's body, then hunted down the herder and shot him dead.

Opium dens operated underground in "China Alley"; above ground cocaine was sold in little packets called bindles. China Alley, located between Minnesota and First Avenue south in the 2600 block, was the scene of hundreds of drug busts in the 1930s.

In 1935, community leaders organized the "Committee of 100" in an attempt to "raise the moral tone of the city." Residents were alarmed at a growing crime rate connected with narcotics, alcohol and prostitution. The committee's goal was to work with law officers to eliminate the sale of alcohol to minors, reduce the narcotics trade and encourage enforcement of laws involving moral issues. The committee was only active for about a year and its effectiveness is unknown, but drug trafficking in Billings did decline in the late 1930s.

Like any rip-roaring western town, Billings had its share of prostitutes and flamboyant madams. Kit Rumley was one of the latter. Rumley ran a well known social club and "sporting house" in Billings during the 1880s. Teddy "Blue" Abbott, a Montana cowboy turned writer, knew Rumley and dubbed her "the first lady of the night."

Rumley's notoriety was nothing in comparison to that of Ollie Warren, who moved to Billings around

## Opium Dens and Sporting Houses

The turn of the century heralded a new crime problem on Billings streets—drug trafficking. In 1909, a Chinese man, Hoo Sue Quoing, was killed in a shootout with police. When the gun fight was over police discovered an opium den in the back of a saloon on Minnesota Avenue. That incident was the opening salvo in long war on drugs like opium, cocaine, morphine, heroin and marijuana.

Chinese residents with connections to a west coast syndicate were at the heart of the drug trade. Organized gangs, called tongs, were active in Billings as early as 1916. One section of town in particular was known for its drug trade.

1897. Warren's story has everything a romance novelist could ask for. She was a beautiful, spunky young woman who graduated from a convent school in Denver. Warren made her way to Billings and began work in the Yegen Brothers general store. There she caught the eye of a young Billings attorney and their love affair led to a business arrangement.

With money from her lawyer friend, Warren opened Billings' most lavish bordello, the Lucky Diamond. It was a smashing success. Warren's admirers deluged her with gifts of jewelry, clothing and fancy horses. She flaunted them all. Wearing an elegant green velvet riding suit and plumed hat, Warren rode through the streets of Billings on a high-stepping black horse.

Warren used some of her profits from the Lucky Diamond to diversify her holdings. She bought the Virginia Hotel in Billings and a ranch in Wyoming. Ollie Warren died in Billings in 1943, nearly 50 years after she began her infamous career here.

It was probably just as well. The heyday of open prostitution in Billings was nearly over. Young men from the area were joining the army and marching off to fight in World War II. Many of them came through Billings, where military officials were appalled at the prevalence of prostitution.

*Ollie Warren.* COURTESY HARRISON G. FAGG

The army wanted Billings' red light district shut down.

Kathryn Wright was a reporter for the *Billings Gazette* at the time. In her book, *Billings, The Magic City and How it Grew*, Wright recalls attending a meeting between a military officer and city officials. She quotes the officer as saying:

"Our health tests have proven that if a potential recruit spends 12 hours in Billings, he's unfit for military service. I am talking about your line of cribs where naked women lean over window sills and entice young boys in for 50 cents or a dollar. Close that south-side line in 24 hours or the military will move in and do it for you."

The city made a half-hearted attempt to close the red light district. But, of course, prostitution didn't disappear. After the war, a south-side house known as Della's flourished for many years. Eventually, street-walkers on Minnesota Avenue took the place of naked women in the cribs.

Somehow, when we look back at the streets of the Old West, the crime and violence tend to seem like entertaining examples of frontier excitement and adventure. A romantic patina obscures the genuine grief and outrage residents experienced. Realistically, people then felt the same as people today when a respected sheriff or a good neighbor was murdered in cold blood. And, Ollie Warren aside, prostitution in the 1890s was no more glamorous a career choice than it is today.

Fortunately, one of modern Billings' most attractive features is its atmosphere of personal safety and low crime. Like other small cities, Billings' crime rates are below national averages. For instance, in the early 1990s, a survey of over 8,000 of the nation's cities showed an average rate of 338 robberies reported for every 100,000 people. Billings had a rate of less than 72 robberies reported per 100,000. Rates for other offenses like homicide, rape, aggravated assault, burglary and auto theft were all significantly lower than the national averages.

According to Billings police, illegal drug activities are behind many of the serious crimes that do occur in Billings. In an echo of the 1930s, drug-trafficking gangs from the West Coast tried to move into Billings in the early 1990s. Hate groups with ties to the Ku Klux Klan also surfaced. But Billings is not an easy place for these groups to get a foothold. Civic leaders and police are quick to respond to the threat of such activities.

New law enforcement programs are being used in Billings to fight crime in an old-fashioned way. A concept called community policing, which is being used in other areas in the United States, assigns specific officers to specific neighborhoods. The officers don't just cruise around in patrol cars looking for signs of trouble. They get out, walk the streets and get to know the people of the neighborhood. Together, residents and police adopt strategies to reduce crime.

Billings police and sheriff department officers are also involved with area schools through programs like D.A.R.E. (Drug Abuse Resistance Education) and Adopt-a-Cop. These programs reach children with a dual message—drugs are for losers and cops are okay. Community policing and school programs are designed to create a partnership between police and citizens. Residents learn peaceful ways to make their neighborhoods safer, and officers get reconnected with the people they serve.

The first community police officer in Billings was Irvin Floth. He was assigned to the neighborhood around Billings South Park in the early 1990s. On his beat, Floth sometimes walks, sometimes drives and sometimes rides a bicycle. Floth helped drive drug dealers out of the neighborhood park simply by sitting on a bench next to suspected dealers. They felt uneasy and left. Residents also made a point of using the park and making the atmosphere good for families and uncomfortable for criminals.

Officer Floth knows residents of his beat by name, especially the kids, and he takes an interest in what going on in their lives. In some ways, Floth illustrates how community policing is law enforcement come full circle. On the other hand, it's probably not the way Liver-Eating Johnson would have handled things.

*Some of the many faces of
the Billings area.*
**Above:** *Putting the finishing
touches on an entry in the
Annual Festival of Trees
charity event.* JAMES WOODCOCK
**Top right:** *A Young man
rapels off the face of the
rimrocks.* BOB ZELLAR
**Right:** *Young Hutterite
women working in the fields
north of Roundup.*
J. MARK KEGANS

**Facing page:** *Heading for
the top of a "twisty" slide is
perfect for a hot summer
day.* BOB ZELLAR

# Calamity Jane

When it comes to romance beating the stuffing out of reality, there's hardly a better story than that of Calamity Jane. There are so many versions of Calamity Jane's life that finding even a portion of the truth is nearly impossible. Historians do agree on a few things. They're almost sure she was born as Martha Jane Canary in Princeton, Missouri around 1852. And, they know she lived the last years of her life in a cabin on Canyon Creek near Billings.

In between, things are pretty murky. It seems young Martha Jane came west with her family to Montana's gold mines around 1864. Sometime after they reached the gold camps, her parents either died or left. Martha Jane may have cared for her brothers and sisters for a time. Some people say she earned her nickname in the camps, because whenever an epidemic of miner's fever or other calamity occurred, Martha Jane would be there working hard to care for the sick.

At any rate, Martha Jane

eventually emerged from the mining camps, without a family, but with a new name. From then on, Calamity Jane roamed the mountain territories and worked a variety of jobs. She claimed to have been an army scout for General George Custer, a stagecoach driver, and a bullwhacker with a freighting firm. Eastern newspaper reporters and novelists wrote stirring tales of Calamity Jane, the beautiful young spitfire who could ride and shoot better than any man, yet was a saintly nurse when illness or misfortune struck.

Calamity said she was once married to Wild Bill Hickok. Others doubt that story, but believe Calamity could have been married—some reports give her as many as 12 husbands. Still others say her involvement with men was more likely prostitution. Calamity did have at least one husband, a man named Clinton Burk (or Burke). There may have been others too. A 1901 article in the *Billings Gazette* refers to "Mrs. R. S. Dorsett, better known as Calamity Jane."

Calamity was very much a part of street life in early Billings. She is mentioned as living on a ranch near town in an 1886 *Billings Gazette* article. In 1895, she bought her Canyon Creek property, where she lived for the next eight years. Around Billings, Calamity is known to have made her living by driving a stagecoach, hauling wood, and cooking. Some people believed she earned extra cash by stealing horses.

In 1893, Buffalo Bill Cody hired her to tour with his Wild West Show. By this time, however, Calamity's hard life had taken a stiff toll on her appearance and abilities. There's speculation that the woman who appeared on posters and in the show was actually a stand-in. In Billings, old-timers defended Calamity Jane as a woman with a heart of gold who would indeed stand by any man down on his luck. But it was tough to recognize the legendary heroine in the foul-mouthed, tobacco-chewing, cigar-smoking, belligerent old drunk who was the real Calamity Jane.

Calamity's sprees frequently got her into trouble with the law. In 1901, a drunken Calamity was thrown in the Billings jail for trying to attack a couple of store clerks with a hatchet. In spite of her orneriness, residents seem to have regarded Calamity with tolerance and a measure of affection. When she boarded a 1903 train for South Dakota without a ticket, passengers took up a collection to pay her fare. Calamity knew she was dying and wanted to get back to Deadwood so she could be buried next to her old friend, Wild Bill. And she was.

After Calamity's death, a Billings woman, Jane Hickok McCormick announced that she was the daughter of Calamity Jane and Wild Bill. McCormick said she had been brought up by a wealthy East Coast family because Calamity realized she couldn't properly raise her own child. To support these claims, McCormick produced a diary supposedly written by Calamity Jane. At the time, it all seemed plausible enough, but modern historians believe the diary was falsified. McCormick lived in Billings until her death in 1951.

# Elixir of the Big Sky

elixir \i-lik'-ser\ n. 1: a) substance held capable of changing base metals into gold; b) a substance held capable of prolonging life indefinitely; c) a cure-all; 2: the essential principle.

...from the definition in Webster's New Collegiate Dictionary

*T*he Montana frontier drew pragmatic idealists—gutsy, sharp-witted dream seekers eager to build better lives. The early settlers believed in the value of progress and change, and looked forward to "taming" nature with hard physical work. Knowing they were headed for a land of danger, violence and uncertainty, they came anyway, because the country seemed to hold such golden promise. Under Montana's big sky, settlers found an exhilarating elixir of freedom, adventure and opportunity.

## New Immigrants

Today, dream seekers are once again moving to Montana with hopes of building better lives. In 1992, national moving companies reported that Montana was a "magnet state", meaning significantly more people moved in than out. The Ryder company listed Billings as the nation's second most popular small city to move to. Today's immigrants often come for very different reasons than the early settlers did.

Many newcomers to Billings are urban refugees, hoping to escape the danger and violence of big city America. They are looking for a place where life is safer, simpler and less frenetic. They don't

*Hutterites at the Farmer's Market.* LARRY MAYER

*Three legged races at North Park.* MICHAEL CRUMMETT

want to "tame" nature so much as to enjoy its unspoiled beauty, and they are far more interested in recreational opportunities than they are in opportunities for hard outdoor labor. Most wouldn't know what to do with a farm or ranch if it were given to them.

## Less Stress

Will these modern dream seekers find what they're looking for? Billings certainly offers them a more relaxed lifestyle. The logistics of everyday life, like shopping or commuting to work are easily managed, and law-abiding citizens still have the upper hand in Billings. The cost of living is relatively low here, but then so are wages. Some of the most successful dream seekers are entrepreneurs who bring their work with them.

Newcomers are pleased to discover that the people of Billings are open and friendly, preserving the tradition of western hospitality. It's common to encounter strangers, and even store clerks, who greet you with a smile. Billings residents tend to be conservative on social issues, but they're also open to new ideas. Ever the pragmatic idealists, the people of Billings often dream big dreams, and then turn them into reality. Projects like the Alberta Bair Theater and ZooMontana reflect an ongoing zest for building a better life.

Even more revealing is the strategic plan adopted by Billings and Yellowstone County in 1991. Work on the plan began when residents pulled their dreams and schemes together into a unified vision for the area's future. The long-range plan charts a course for the future in basic industries, human services, education, infrastructure, culture, and tourism.

Billings business and community leaders have a history of working together to solve problems, including volatile issues like air pollution. When sulfur dioxide emissions from local industries reached maximum legal limits, citizens groups, local government officials and industry representatives agreed to form the Billings/Laurel Air Quality Technical Committee. The committee monitors sulfur dioxide lev-

# Entrepreneurial Energy

Billings has always produced and attracted its share of entrepreneurs. In 1882, the Yegens were a Swiss immigrant family who started out with a small bakery and gradually emerged as some of the city's most prominent business people. In 1918, a young Irish immigrant named Barry O'Leary started a sewer-digging business with a bicycle, a pick and a shovel. He branched out into ready-mixed concrete in 1922, and eventually O'Leary and his wife owned the largest concrete construction firm in the region.

Today, entrepreneurial energy continues to be at work here. At least 26 companies headquartered in the city market products and services nationally or internationally. Those produced here include wooden kaleidoscopes, quilting frames, surgical supplies and commercial cabinets.

Billings' Cream of the West company, owned by area rancher Bud Luethold, sells three varieties of hot cereal in 30 states and overseas. Luethold bought the company in 1987, but the original Cream of the West cereal was developed around 1916 when a Montana rancher cooked up some wheat porridge for her cowboys. It was so tasty that a visiting salesman rushed back to Billings and began commercial production.

Geo-Research is a Billings-based firm that produces sophisticated computer mapping software for clients throughout the world. Kampgrounds of America has been headquartered in Billings since the company was founded here in 1962. KOA is considered one of the top 100 franchisers in the United States.

Americlean is another franchising corporation based in Billings. The company got its start here in 1979, when brothers Bob and Jim Pearson bought a small carpet-cleaning business. Their experiments with better ways to clean carpeting eventually led to methods of restoring household and office furnishings damaged by fire or water. Today, Americlean specializes in disaster restoration, and has franchised operations in 21 states.

Good airline connections and modern communications technology like fax machines and modems help these Billings-based businesses stay in touch with their clients, wherever they may be. Freelance professionals like writers, consultants, and brokers also use technology and air travel to tap into the global marketplace while living and working in Billings.

els in the valley and looks for ways to reduce them. One response by industry was Conoco's 1991 construction of a $140 million coker plant which helped reduce pollutants released by its Billings refinery.

Because of the city's ability to mobilize community resources to solve local problems, the National Civic League named Billings one of ten All America Cities in 1992. Billings was also recognized by a 1991 *Money* magazine survey as the sixth most livable city in the United States.

Recreational opportunities are an important part of Billings' popularity. At Cobb Field, fans root for two hometown American Legion baseball teams and the minor league Billings Mustangs, a farm team for the Cincinnati Reds. Major league players George Brett, Paul O'Neil, Tom Browning, Joe Oliver and Glenn Sutko all played for the Billings Mustangs.

Golf has been played in Billings since the 1920s. Back then duffers used the prairie for a fairway and mixed road oil with sand to form the "greens." Nowadays, Billings has four public and five private courses, including some of the best professionally designed courses in the region.

Billings' sunny days and moderate climate are an asset to baseball fans, golfers and other outdoor enthusiasts. Many winter storms and cold waves bypass Billings altogether, and frequent thaws prevent the snow that does fall from piling up. In January and February, the peak months for winter weather, warm winds called chinooks (meaning snow-eaters) blow in from the southwest bringing welcome periods of spring-like temperatures.

Summer days range from warm to hot, but nights are almost always cool. In July, the hottest month, the average high is 87 degrees Fahrenheit and the average low is 56 degrees. Year-round low humidity makes both hot and cold temperatures feel more comfortable.

## Enjoying the Great Outdoors

For many people, Billings' livability is greatly enhanced by its proximity to recreation in the great Montana outdoors. Excellent opportunities for hiking, biking, hunting, downhill and cross-country skiing can be found within an easy drive of Billings. Immediately beyond the city are some of Montana's legendary wide open spaces with rolling plains, steep hills and flat tablelands.

Within an hour's drive are the Pryor, Bull and Beartooth mountain ranges. The Beartooth Highway, from Red Lodge to Cooke City, offers spectacular mountain scenery. Yellowstone National Park is only three hours away. The Big Horn, Madison, Stillwater, Boulder, Musselshell and Yellowstone rivers are favorite locations for trout fishing, canoeing, kayaking and rafting.

The great outdoors also holds many direct links to Montana's history. Pompeys Pillar, with William Clark's signature carved into its side, is just east of Billings. The Little Bighorn Battlefield, site of the Plains Indians' bloody victory over Lt. Col. George Custer, is an hour's drive southeast of Billings.

Fifteen miles west of the city is the site of another battle in which Chief Joseph led a band of Nez Perce Indians to victory over the U.S. Cavalry under the command of Colonel S. D. Sturgis. The home of Chief Plenty Coups, last chief of the Crows, is preserved 35 miles south of Billings on the Crow Reservation.

Right in Billings, the Black Otter Trail along the north Rims commemorates the death of another Crow Chief, Black Otter. The trail also passes the old Boothill Cemetery and the gravesite of Yellowstone Kelly, a famous frontier scout who requested burial overlooking the Yellowstone River. Across the valley are the Pictograph Indian Caves containing prehistoric paintings by the area's aboriginal people.

Residents can also experience nature-in-the-raw on the city's doorstep. Four of the 48 parks within the city lie along the Yellowstone River. Two

Moon, Coulson, and Riverfront and Riverfront East parks provide hundreds of acres of undeveloped land and serve as refuges for both wildlife and "humanlife." Two Moon Park on Billings' east side is a paradise for birds and bird watchers. Over 200 species of birds have been sighted in this 150-acre park.

Riverfront Park, on South Billings Boulevard, has hiking, biking and equestrian trails winding through nearly 400 acres of wooded river bottom. Coulson Park is part of the old Coulson townsite. Its 80 acres are mostly grassy opens with beautiful views of the river and southeastern rimrocks.

Unifying all these parks is the Yellowstone River. The edges of Billings have crept close to the river, but flood plain restrictions prohibit development directly along its banks. A float trip down the river from Duck Creek bridge west of Billings to Coulson Park reveals only brief glimpses of civilization to mar the river's scenic beauty. On the other hand, river-bottom residents like deer, eagles, blue heron, and white pelicans are easy to spot.

As part of the city/county strategic plan, efforts are underway to further protect the river and its environs from development while also making it more accessible to the public. The dream is to create a continuous nature park and trail system along the river throughout Yellowstone County as part of a comprehensive system of trails for the Billings area. It's a complicated venture, but the dream seekers behind it have an advantage: They're working in a city known for turning big ideas into reality.

It's hard to overstate the river's importance to Billings and the valley. The Yellowstone shaped the valley and made it fertile. Water from the river irrigates farms, lawns and gardens, and provides drinking water for residents. Industry utilizes river water to operate its factories.

Residents can refresh their psyches by slipping down to the river's banks or riding her current. In the end, it's probably this remarkable intimacy between the realities of modern life and the restorative powers of nature that define Billings' quality of life.

*I*n the evening, Billings glitters in the valley like a shard of the brilliant night sky toppled to earth. The silent, stone-faced rimrocks stand forever guard, ordered to their posts by the impudent river—the impudent laughing Yellowstone, who slips away from her own sentinels to dance with the moon and sing lusty night songs with the yellow-eyed coyotes.

On her banks, the cottonwoods whisper scandalous tales among themselves while the blue heron and mule-eared deer wisely hold their tongues. Inhabitants of the sky-shard city drink in the river and her antics, her wild friends, mountain parents, and prairie kin. They are all part of the elixir of big sky country.

LARRY MAYER

# For Further Reading

Bramlett, Jim. *Ride for the High Points: The Real Story of Will James.* Missoula: Mountain Press Publishing Co., 1987.

Cooper, Myrtle D. *From Tent Town to City: A Chronological History of Billings, Montana, 1882–1935.* Billings: Myrtle D. Cooper, 1981.

Ralston, J.K. *The Voice of the Curlew,* as told to John A. Popovich. Billings: J.K. Ralston Studio, Inc., 1986.

West, Carroll Van. *Images of Billings: A Photographic History.* Billings: Western Heritage Press, 1990.

Winks, Robin W. *Frederick Billings—A Life.* Oxford University Press Inc., 1991

Wright, Kathryn. *Historic Homes of Billings.* Billings & Helena: Falcon Press, 1981.

Wright, Kathryn. *Billings: The Magic City and How It Grew.* 3rd ed. Billings: K.H. Wright, 1981.

Typewritten bound script. *Billings Pioneers.* Parmly Billings Library.

# Index

Snidow, T.A. 81
Steamboats 15
Streetcars 71
Strikes the Arrow Rock 40
Stuart, James 28
Sugar beet industry 63–66
Sugar beets *63, 65*
Sully, Gen. Alfred 15
Sweet Medicine, Cheyenne
   prophet 24, 25

Taylor, Muggins 95–96
Telephone service 71
Terry, General Alfred H. 36
Theaters 83–85
Tipi rings *8*
Tourism industry 78–79
Two Bears Lake *68*
Two Moon, Chief 25, 37

Two Moon Park 16, 107

Vigilantes 96

Wallowing Bull, Dallas *23*
Warren, Ollie 97–98, *98*
Webb, Sheriff John T. 96
Western Heritage Center 59,
   *72,* 87
Wright, Kathryn 98

Yale Oil 74
Yegen Brothers 108
Yegen Brothers Implement
   Company *91*
Yegen Brothers Store *60*
Yellowstone Art Center *88,* 90
Yellowstone County Museum
   87

Yellowstone National Park 16,
   32, 40, 78, 106
Yellowstone River *12,* 12–16,
   *14,* 17, 55, 58, 106–107, 107
Yellowstone, The (steamboat)
   15
Yellowtail Dam 39
Yerkes, A.K. 49, 50

ZooGrass Festival 90, *92*
ZooMontana 90